F. A. Gore Ouseley

A Treatise on Musical form and General Composition

F. A. Gore Ouseley

A Treatise on Musical form and General Composition

ISBN/EAN: 9783337084790

Printed in Europe, USA, Canada, Australia, Japan

Cover: Foto ©Thomas Meinert / pixelio.de

More available books at **www.hansebooks.com**

Clarendon Press Series

MUSICAL FORM

AND

GENERAL COMPOSITION

OUSELEY

London

HENRY FROWDE

OXFORD UNIVERSITY PRESS WAREHOUSE

AMEN CORNER, E.C.

Clarendon Press Series

A TREATISE

MUSICAL FORM AND GENERAL COMPOSITION

BY THE

REV. SIR F. A. GORE OUSELEY, BART., M.A., MUS. DOC.

PROFESSOR OF MUSIC IN THE UNIVERSITY OF OXFORD

SECOND EDITION

Oxford

AT THE CLARENDON PRESS

M.DCCC.LXXXVI

PREFACE TO THE FIRST EDITION.

THE present Treatise is intended to supply an acknowledged want, and to be a sequel to the Author's works on Harmony and Counterpoint.

He has been so often asked to write a treatise on the subject of Form, to serve as a text-book, that he is encouraged to hope that the following pages may prove useful, and supply a want that is certainly felt.

He had at one time intended to have written a few chapters on Instrumentation, either as an Appendix to the present Volume, or as a separate work. But subsequent consideration has satisfied him that the excellent treatises of Berlioz and Kastner, of which the former has been translated into English, amply suffice for the instruction of students in the art of writing for various instruments.

Though the Author feels that he can honestly say that he has spared no pains to render this Treatise on Form as perfect as possible, he yet knows that there must be omissions and blemishes in it ; and he therefore hopes that if it should ever reach a second edition he may have the benefit of friendly criticism to aid him in the task of improving it.

October, 1874.

PREFACE TO THE SECOND EDITION.

In the eleven years which have elapsed since the publication of the former edition of this Treatise, some not unfriendly criticisms of the work have appeared, containing valuable suggestions of which the Author has thankfully availed himself in preparing the present Edition for the Press. Not a few inaccuracies (fortunately of no great importance however) have also been detected, which have now been corrected. In the Fifth and Ninth Chapters some considerable changes and additions have been made, which will, it is hoped, increase the usefulness and completeness of the work. The Author ventures therefore to express his earnest wish that the Treatise, in its present amended form, may prove as acceptable to musical students as he has reason to believe it has been hitherto.

December, 1885.

TABLE OF CONTENTS.

CONTENTS.

CHAPTER XII.

CHAPTER XIII.

LIST OF EXAMPLES.

THE PRINCIPLES

OF

FORM AND GENERAL COMPOSITION

IN MUSIC.

CHAPTER I.

Introductory.

1. IT is often thought that, when a student has thoroughly mastered the theory and practice of Harmony and Counterpoint, and can consequently harmonise any given melody correctly and variously, and introduce such "learned" devices as imitations and canons into his work, then he is a trained musician and composer, and has only to apply his acquirements in order to enrich the world with new and excellent compositions of his own. No mistake can be greater than this : it might as well be supposed that a man who had learnt grammar and orthography might thereupon set up for an epic poet, or become a writer of satirical essays, without further training. For in truth Harmony and Counterpoint are, after all, but that preparatory study of the technical rules without which the edifice cannot be reared ; but it requires architectural skill and experience in addition to form them into a really good musical structure.

B

2. This architectural skill and experience cannot be imparted entirely by books. In some degree it is a natural gift, possessed by certain persons, and denied to others. And just as we are told that "Poeta nascitur non fit," so it may be said of a composer, that the requisite genius must be born in him, and cannot be acquired by study. Still, as there are different degrees of genius and of aptitude among men, so it may well be argued that any one who has the least musical perception can tell what latent sparks of inventive musical fire he may possess. And if so, it is obvious that cultivation and study will tend to develope those hidden resources and quicken the creative powers. A knowledge of Harmony and Counterpoint is the first and most indispensable requisite for such a purpose; but, after all, Harmony and Counterpoint are not enough by themselves to enable the student to accomplish the toilsome ascent of the musical Parnassus. The power of originating new melodies and of combining them together so as to form a consistent whole is the first faculty of which any newly-awakened genius will avail itself. The Harmonic and Contrapuntal treatment of such melodies may be regarded as absolutely necessary if the composer aspires to climb the highest peaks. But the origination of melody is after all the true act of composition; while the correct way of using and combining new melodies is one of the highest walks of art. And this is exactly where the power and importance of symmetry and rhythmic balance make themselves felt, and from this consideration we must deduce the whole theory and practice of MUSICAL FORM, which is to be the principal subject of this treatise.

Our first care then must be to investigate the laws of *melody*.

CHAPTER II.

Of Melody.

1. A GENERAL definition of Melody would describe it as "a succession of single musical sounds arranged in a certain order both as to pitch and as to rhythm, so as to produce an agreeable impression on the ear." But this, although a correct general definition, would be insufficient as a guide either to the composition or to the analysis of particular melodies, unless accompanied by many special rules and explanations.

2. Indeed it may well be doubted whether the composition of new melodies, worthy of the name, can be acquired by rules or definitions at all. The most that such artificial aids can do is to enable the student to avoid glaring errors in his own works and to detect them in the works of others. The faculty of inventing a new melody is a *gift*, as we have already observed; it must come, as it were, spontaneously into the composer's head. In this fact indeed it is obviously akin to poetry; for although you may teach a man the rules of versification or of melody, yet you cannot thereby make him a poet or a composer, unless he have also those natural dispositions for the work which constitute him what is commonly called *a genius*. Both poetry and melody appeal to the emotions of the hearer for their effect; and no hearer will recognise or respond to their appeal, unless it have its origin in the emotions or passions of the composer or poet himself. Such emotional powers of influencing others through the medium of the arts cannot be acquired by study, unless the creative germ of them be already there. But if it *be* there,—if the student be gifted, that is, with even a single spark of poetic or musical fire,—then indeed the rules of art can fan that spark into a flame, and enable the latent gifts to develope themselves into real artistic powers. And these powers may fairly be called *influences*, because the sister arts may be regarded as a kind of language wherein, so to express it, soul speaks to soul; and if the language of art be not understood, it must be because either the hearer is deaf or the speaker mispronounces his words. In other terms, the true criterion of art is the effect it produces on an intelligent hearer; without this effect all the labour expended on it may be said to have been utterly thrown away.

3. These remarks do not apply so much to Harmony as they do to Melody; for any man may learn how to harmonise correctly by a diligent study of the principles and rules of that branch of the art, and by the aid of qualified instructors. It does not require the gift of genius to make a man a good harmonist; although it must be confessed that without that gift he will never be able to strike out *new effects* in Harmony. But in the case of Melody no amount of study can teach an unmusical man to invent a new tune, although he may learn to find out the faults in an old one or to copy its merits.

4. Again, Counterpoint and the art of Fugue can be mastered thoroughly by dint of laborious application; even fairly good fugues may be produced without any real musical inspiration, though of course they would be all the better were that important element present. Given the melodies, any studious musical scholar may learn to supply the harmonies, the counterpoints, and even the instrumentation. But when he has done all this he will only have proved himself a good *arranger*,

not a *composer*, inasmuch as the very foundation on which all his superstructure has been reared is not his own at all.

5. From what has just been said it follows that, from one point of view, Melody is the most important and necessary of the elements which go to make a good composer. A man may be a thoroughly accomplished musician, an excellent critic, an admirable arranger, a perfect sight-reader, a brilliant player, an exquisite singer, a steady accompanyist, or an experienced conductor; any or all of these things he may be; but if in addition to his other qualifications he is not able to compose good original melodies, he has no claim to be considered a true composer.

6. On the other hand there is reason to believe that the power of originating good melodies is latent in many persons who are ignorant of their own faculties, and have therefore never cultivated them. In all such cases an acquaintance with the rules of art and a careful study of the best models will tend to draw out and make available that hidden power; and it is principally to such persons that this portion of our treatise will be found useful.

7. Moreover it will surely be admitted to be a manifest advantage to any lover of music if he can analyse any melody he may hear, so as to be able to judge of its merits or demerits. To this object also this treatise pays attention, and will therefore, it is hoped, be helpful to the student.

8. A melody, if it is to produce a pleasing effect on the ear, must be written in some definite tonality. The intervals of which it consists must form part of some regular scale. In ancient times, long before the invention of Harmony, scales were more varied, and also less satisfactory than they are now. The consideration of the Ancient Greek scales, and likewise of Oriental systems, is foreign to the

purpose of this work.   But of the so-called Gregorian scales it may
be said that they are founded on the Greek tetrachords, and named
after the ancient Greek modes.   They consist, as do our modern diatonic
scales, of tones and semitones, and they also agree with our scales in
only admitting two semitones in the octave.   But they differ from our
modern scales in the *place* of their semitones: instead of placing them
always between the 3rd and 4th, and the 7th and 8th degrees, as in
the modern major mode, or between the 2nd and 3rd, and the 7th and
8th, as in our present minor mode, the ancient musicians of Europe
placed their semitones very variously, as will be seen by the annexed
diagram, in which the various Gregorian scales or modes are placed in
order, with their Greek names attached, and divided into their two
divisions of *authentic* and *plagal*, with the principal note (called in ancient
days the Dominant) in larger characters by way of distinction.

AUTHENTIC.	PLAGAL.
Dorian, or first mode.	Hypodorian, or second mode.
D ef g a bc D.	a bc D ef g a.
Phrygian, or third mode.	Hypophrygian, or fourth mode.
Ef g a bc d E.	bc d Ef g a b.
Lydian, or fifth mode.	Hypolydian, or sixth mode.
F g a bc d eF.	c d eF g a bc.
Mixolydian, or seventh mode.	Hypomixolydian, or eighth mode.
G a bc d ef G.	d ef G a bc d.

A line has been drawn under the letters indicating the interval of
a semitone in the above table.

9. It will be observed that none of these scales coincide exactly
with our major and minor modes.   The second mode looks like a minor
scale, but the principal note is D instead of A.   So again, the sixth mode

looks like a major scale, but the principal note is not C but F. Melodies written in any of these scales have the effect of being, as we may say, in no particular key; and if we attempt to harmonise them, we are obliged for the most part to begin and end our harmonies in a different key from that which seems to prevail in the course of the piece. Although then it must be admitted that many melodies of this kind have a certain wild and crude charm of their own, yet no one in the present day would feel inclined to compose in such imperfect and unsatisfactory scales. As soon as the modern system of tonality was discovered and introduced to the musical world some three hundred years ago, all new melodies were made to conform to it, and every piece of music required a proper close on the tonic. This then is an essential requisite in every fresh melody; it must be written in some major or minor key, closing on the key note, with a regular cadence from dominant to tonic.

10. The next fundamental principle which regulates the production of good melody is that of *Symmetry*. There can be no doubt that the more regularly balanced the members of a melody are, the more easily intelligible it will be. In mediæval times the only symmetry observed was that of the poetry to which the music was set, except indeed in the case of dance-music, which necessarily had a musical rhythm of its own, but of which we unfortunately know very little. Ever since the introduction of the signs for notes of various lengths (by Franco, in the middle of the twelfth century), an increasing attention to and appreciation of musical symmetry and rhythm have made themselves felt: and no melody can be satisfactory to modern ears in which these conditions are not duly fulfilled.

11. Every regular melody may be divided into *Periods*, *Phrases*, and *Strains*. These may be said to constitute the Prosody of music.

Let us analyse a fragment of melody in order to explain this. The following is the beginning of the Huntsman's Chorus in Weber's Opera "Der Freyschütz":—

This, taken altogether, is a *Period*—a complete sentence ending with a full stop. It is divided into two *Phrases* of equal length. Each of these phrases is subdivided into two equal *Strains*. The strains are marked by brackets placed over the notes ; the phrases by longer brackets placed under them. Here we obviously have perfect symmetry and regularity throughout the whole period.

12. Symmetry may exist, however, without melody. Here, for instance, there is no melody, but yet there is perfect symmetry ; for

we have a period of eight bars divided into two equal and similar phrases, and each phrase consisting, as it were, of two equal and similar strains, as indicated by the brackets. But this cannot be called *music*, because there is no melody at all. To make music of it, it will be necessary to build a melody on this symmetrical but monotonous basis. This may be done as follows—

The symmetrical arrangement here remains as before: the value of the notes is not altered: the division of the period into phrases and strains is exactly the same: but there has been superadded a real melody, and it has been made so by varying the pitch of the notes. The great principle of definite scale and key, without which no melody can exist, has here been carried out. In the present instance our melody is in the key of C major. A melody need not be kept rigidly in one key; but it should begin and end in it always; and in the case of so exceedingly short a melody as this one, which is only eight bars long, no room is left for any departure from the key in which it begins and ends. Indeed, so simple is the tonality of this tune, that it can be accompanied by the descending scale of C, excepting indeed the last note but one; thus—

or still better by adopting the bass figure, which occurs in the last bar but one throughout, in this way—

13. But let us now proceed to analyse this melody a little more narrowly. It consists of the following strains:—

No. 1.

No. 2.

No. 3.

No. 4.

Now it is noticeable that of these four strains none, except the last, wholly satisfies the ear: there is always a craving for some new thing to follow, until we get to the end of No. 4. And why is this? Simply because there is no full stop in the sentence till then; no perfect cadence or close. Let us then consider this matter of cadences or closes with reference to the construction of a melody. The meaning of cadences in relation to Harmony, together with the necessary rules for this aspect of them, is fully explained and discussed in the author's "Treatise on Harmony," Chapters XIII and XIV. But purely melodic cadences, where no accompanying harmony is present, vary somewhat from the cadences of harmony, being more numerous, and of a different nature in some respects.

14. A melodic perfect cadence must end with the key-note, preceded by either the dominant itself, or some note belonging to the dominant chord.

It must also generally fall on the first, or strong beat of the bar.

To both these rules there are exceptions, but they are of comparatively rare occurrence.

Let us now apply them to the four strains of which the above melody consists.

In No. 1 the cadence is not perfect, because it goes from the tonic C to the dominant G, and also because it ends on the last or weak beat of the bar.

In No. 2, although the cadence falls on the strong beat, yet it does not end on the tonic, but on the leading note, or major third of the dominant: it is therefore also an imperfect cadence.

In No. 3, although the cadence goes from the dominant to the tonic, yet it is not a perfect melodic cadence, inasmuch as it falls on the weak or second beat of the bar.

But in No. 4 the cadence not only goes from dominant to tonic, but also falls on the strong beat at the beginning of the last bar: this then is a perfect cadence, or full stop; the ear is satisfied; it requires nothing more to follow. Therefore, as far as it goes, this little period of melody, short as it is, is absolutely complete.

15. The next point to observe is the correspondence which exists between the four strains.

The first is repeated, *very nearly* in the same intervals, by the third, only at a pitch a fifth lower. As the first goes from the tonic to the dominant, so does the third go from the subdominant to the tonic. The correspondence between the second and fourth strains is of a different sort, depending entirely on the cadences. That of the

second strain is the same as to symmetry of rhythm with that of the
fourth, for they both end with one note on the down beat; but,
whereas the second leads away from the key, the fourth strain leads
back to it; whereas the second appears to ask, "Here I am, how
shall I get home?" the fourth strain answers the enquiry by em-
phatically crying, "Come this way, now you are at home again."

16. By adding various harmonies, of course, the meaning of the
melody may be considerably varied. For instance, the half-close at the
end of the second strain may be thus converted into a real modulation
into the key of G major, or of A minor; thus—

But what we have chiefly to attend to at present is the melody alone, apart from all harmonic considerations.

17. Now, if it were wished to lengthen this little melody, the first operation would be to get rid of the full close, or perfect cadence at the end of the period, or at least so to modify or weaken it as to destroy its finality, and thus to induce the ear to expect something to come after it: otherwise the effect of the whole piece would be rather that of two distinct melodies heard in succession than that of one melody divided into two periods. Instead, therefore, of making the last bars end as they do at present, it will be necessary to alter the close somewhat as follows:

This is now no longer a perfect melodic cadence, for it neither ends on the key-note, nor does it finish on the strong beat of the bar.

It is now fit to receive some such addition as the following:

18. If this new period be analysed, it will be seen to consist, like the former one, of eight bars, divided into two equal phrases of four bars, these again being subdivided into strains of two bars each; so that, in point of symmetry, it is as complete and regular as its predecessor. In all other respects, however, it differs from it altogether. For the two strains which make up its former phrase are almost alike, except as to pitch, wherein they differ by an ascent of a whole tone. The second phrase contains two utterly dissimilar strains, of which the former is somewhat of an imitation of the preceding strains, while the latter comes to a close on the note G. But here the question arises, what sort of G have we here? Is it a dominant or a tonic G? In other words, has a modulation taken place into the key of G, or are we still in that of C? This question is at once answered by the occurrence of F♯ twice in the period, which note forms no part of the scale of C, but belongs to that of G, of which it is the leading note. We have then modulated into the key of G. But have we come to a full close in that key? Is the ear satisfied with the end to which this new period has arrived? or does it crave something more? Most assuredly it asks for more, and for two reasons; first because the concluding note is not on the strong but on the weak beat of the bar; and secondly and chiefly because the impression of the original key of C is not entirely effaced, and therefore a trace of the dominant character of the G still remains. The melody therefore is still incomplete; and it may be completed in two ways: either by composing an entirely new period to succeed the last one, which shall end regularly with a full close on C; or by repeating the first melody by way of conclusion with its original full close. Taking the latter of these alternatives, the completed melody will be as follows, consisting altogether of three equal periods of eight bars each.

19. But most melodies are somewhàt less symmetrical in their
structure than the foregoing example. And music has this in common
with versification, that a slight departure from absolute regularity of
form may be sometimes a relief to the ear and an improvement of the
effect, while at the same time the strictest symmetry is usually
observed, and any exceptions to it should be made and guarded by
the most careful attention to the requirements of good taste.

It has become, unfortunately, a fashion with young composers at
the present day, in far too many cases, to disparage regular melody,
and to compose pieces, sometimes of great length, in which it is
hard, or even impossible, to detect any air (or regular melody)
whatsoever. Against such a system of composition it is high time
to protest. Music without melody may fitly be likened to a painting
without an outline, or to a poem without any definite meaning.

In defence of this modern craze against regular melody, it is
sometimes urged that all the best successions of notes have been
exhausted in the works of the great Composers, so that it is impossible
to write a good air now-a-days without being guilty of plagiarism.
But that this is a false assertion is sufficiently proved by the fact

that new melodies *are* produced, even in these latter days, which are both original and pleasing. Doubtless, as time goes on, and more melodies are invented, the difficulty of producing good new ones increases. But such is the marvellous number of possible permutations of the notes from which melodies may be constructed, that it will be many years indeed before that difficulty becomes insurmountable. It is to be feared, in fact, that the real reason why young composers affect to disparage and despise regular melody is simply because they are unable to produce it themselves.

20. The above melody is absolutely regular, as we have shown. Every period is divided into equal and similar phrases, and each phrase is composed of equal and similar strains. But a strain may consist of three bars instead of two; or a phrase may contain three strains instead of four or two; or again, a period may be composed of three phrases instead of two or four. The melodies resulting from the above combinations will be less symmetrical and regular than those we have been hitherto considering; but they may be very beautiful notwithstanding.

21. "God save the Queen" may be cited as a remarkably good instance of a melody of a slightly irregular kind. Indeed it is so endeared to us by old associations and patriotic feelings, that we do not easily recognise its departures from the normal form. Yet it is essentially an irregular melody. It is divided into two periods, but they are of unequal length. The former period consists of three strains of two bars each. The latter may be divided into two phrases of four bars, each of these phrases being divisible into strains of half that length—

Now the **former period** rather gives the idea of being an expansion of a regular four-bar phrase of two strains, formed by the interpolation of an additional **strain,** inserted between the two others and moulded as a counterpart to the first. **Thus**

is the opening strain;

is the second or interpolated strain, of which the rhythm is obviously the same in all respects. The third strain,

which forms a perfect close on the tonic, is somewhat different in rhythm from its two predecessors. And it is a somewhat noticeable fact that the irregularity of the whole period in the matter of symmetry takes off somewhat from the absolute perfection of this full close and leads the ear to expect some sort of continuation. Thus one irregularity of construction in this case neutralises the effect of the other. Consequently the beauty of the melody as a whole remains unimpaired. In the second period the first thing which we observe is the rhythm of the first two strains, which is the same as that of the opening strains of the former period, thus securing unity of effect in the whole air. These strains are also similar to one another in the order or succession of intervals, except that the second is pitched one degree lower in the scale than the first, thus

The third strain is altogether unlike the rest, and is clearly to be regarded as a connecting link, or rather as a preparation for the final close which follows it. These two concluding strains make up this phrase.

The air is on the whole a very good example of an irregular melody.

22. It sometimes happens that the same bar forms the close of one period and the beginning of another. In this case the adjacent periods *overlap*, and the whole melody is consequently one bar shorter than perfect symmetry would require. It is however quite possible to construct a melody containing this peculiarity, which shall not produce a bad effect. Here is an example taken from Reicha's "Traité de Mélodie." It consists of two periods of four bars each, which overlap one another by half a bar, and yet do not by any means produce an unpleasant result.

First period of four bars.

Second period of four bars.

Such melodies as the above must always be to a certain extent lame and unsatisfactory, nor can they ever produce so good an effect as those in which the requirements of perfect symmetry are enforced: still the above example, and many others which might be quoted, suffice to show the use which may be made of such compositions, and it is obvious that they afford a valuable element of variety.

23. Perhaps the best and commonest instance of this particular sort of melody is to be found in an ordinary English single or double

chant. For example, take the well-known chant in E, by Lord Mornington.

As usually written, of course it appears to consist of four phrases, of which the first and third contain three bars each, while the second and fourth contain four apiece. This apparently limping and anomalous structure may probably be explained by supposing that the fourth and eleventh bars do as it were double duty ; serving both as closes and commencements of adjacent phrases. Thus

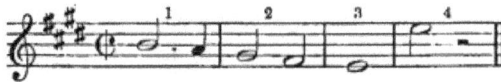

may be regarded as a phrase of four bars. Starting again with the same fourth bar, the second phrase comes out as follows—

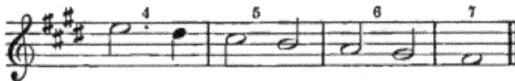

which is perfectly regular, and forms the conclusion of the first period of the chant with an imperfect cadence, or half-close, on the fifth of the dominant chord.   If the third phrase be treated in the same way as the first, the result is

which may be regarded as a regular and symmetrical fragment of melody, four bars in length. Then lastly, regarding the eleventh bar as being not only the concluding bar of the third phrase, but also the commencement of the fourth, the conclusion of the chant will be as follows—

than which nothing can be more regular, as it is a phrase of four bars ending with a full close on the tonic. So that in this case a melody of fourteen bars produces virtually the effects of a more regular one of sixteen: and what makes this explanation of the construction of an English double chant more probable is the fact that the notes which are here supposed to do double duty, and to act in two capacities at once, are always *reciting notes* (i. e. notes of indefinite length, on which long pauses are generally made), and are therefore exceptionally well adapted for the purpose.

24. But chants are by no means the only common cases of melodies in which phrases or periods may be said to overlap. It often happens that in a duet, or other concerted piece, where the voices or instruments come in with their respective melodic periods in succession to one

another, the same bar forms the conclusion of one period and the beginning of another—for instance,

Other examples will be given at the end of this volume, to which we refer the student.

25. Other cases where the same thing occurs may be found in fugues, canons, and other imitative or contrapuntal compositions. Here is a fugue subject of Handel's—

Handel does not scruple to bring in the answer to this subject in the fourth bar, which bar also concludes the original melody. So the phrases overlap, and the bar does double duty, thus—

&c.

This is so common in fugal works, that it will be needless to give more instances at present.

26. Another large class of melodies are irregular on account of certain interpolated strains which separate phrase from phrase, and period from period. These interpolations are of various kinds. Sometimes they are simple prolongations of a phrase by the addition of an extra bar or two, which generally bears some analogy to what goes before (as is the case with the first part of "God save the Queen," already referred to). Sometimes they take the form of an echo or repetition of particular phrases or strains. Such echoes or repetitions have often a very good effect when they occur in the accompaniment to a song, or as a contrasting orchestral effect in pieces for a full band. The following melody from Reicha is a perfectly regular and

symmetrical one of eight bars, divided into two equal phrases, each phrase consisting of two strains of equal length. The former phrase ends with an imperfect cadence, while the latter finishes with a full close.

This may be made perhaps more interesting by repeating the second and fourth strains in a different octave, and thus producing a kind of echo.

Or again, sometimes a kind of premonitory strain is prefixed to a period by way of preparation. Those who are familiar with Leslie's charming Trio a Canone, "O memory," will remember the emphatic way in which he brings in each voice with a preliminary exclamation before the regular melody is commenced. This is really a most effective instance of the kind of interpolation which we have been considering.

E

27. All the melodies hitherto considered have been short and simple. But it will be easily seen that some additional rules are required when longer and more complicated compositions have to be analysed from a melodic point of view. If period be added to period, and phrase piled upon phrase, without any order as to pitch, length, rhythm, or modulation, no good result can ever be obtained. There must be intelligent design in order to secure the attention, interest, and comprehension of the listener. And the first consideration should be *symmetry of rhythm* between the periods. It is a very general rule that every period should be followed by a companion, or answering period, with exactly the same rhythm as itself. The melodies hitherto quoted have been all, more or less, constructed on this model. Their periods for the most part run in couples. Each couple may differ from other couples as to rhythm; though the variety of good rhythmical forms is by no means great. The most satisfactory periods are those which consist of four, eight, or sixteen bars. The next best are those consisting of three, six, or twelve bars. Periods formed of other numbers of bars generally produce a limping or halting effect on the mind, and should not be taken as models. At the same time a few good examples may be found of melodies containing periods or phrases of five bars; when such is the case such periods or phrases should always be accompanied by a similar companion. As an instance of a melody thus formed, none perhaps can be found more successful than the old French air "Charmante Gabrielle," which consists of two periods, the former containing six bars, while the latter is composed of two companion phrases of five bars each.

In this, as in many other instances, it is mainly the form in which the versification of the words is cast which renders the irregular rhythm of the music tolerable. On the whole the student will do well to avoid in his compositions all phrases or periods of five or seven bars, and confine himself to those of four, eight, or sixteen, in preference to all others.

28. The next consideration is the proper combination of unity and variety in the matter of modulation. If every period in an extended melody began and ended with the tonic, or even with any note in the tonic harmony, a most insufferable monotony would inevitably be produced. To avoid this result, it is absolutely necessary to vary the keys of the different periods, by the introduction of judicious modulations or progressions; only taking care always to begin and end the whole melody in its principal key, and if possible to end it on the key-note itself. At the same time it is very necessary to guard against changing the key so often as to obscure or lose sight of the original key. If this original key be lost to the memory of the hearer, all unity of design is sacrificed. About half-way through an extended melody it is usual and desirable to come to a full close in some nearly related key, such as the dominant, or the relative minor or major. This rests the ear without giving the effect of final completion, and thus prepares the way for the remainder of the tune. And great care should be taken that each period should flow easily out of its

predecessor, without any violent break in the tonality; otherwise a jerky and disconnected effect would be produced, which ought to be carefully avoided.

29. In the next place there is a great distinction between vocal and instrumental melody. Instrumental melody may range over a larger compass of notes than vocal; it may indulge in distant skips and awkward intervals, which are utterly inadmissible in music for voices. Again, vocal music is very dependent on the words to which it is set, and of which it should be the exponent. The emotional character of the words should govern the style of the melody. No melody set to words can be considered good, if it does not agree in all respects with the sentiments it is meant to convey. It is true indeed that melody cannot express very definite ideas by itself: apart from words, all that it can do is to excite certain emotions, *analogous* to the more obvious ones which the words alone can define. Thus it can intensify the effect of poetry, although it never can usurp its place. But such intensification can only be secured by suiting the style of the music to the idea imparted by the words to which it is set. Purely instrumental music is of course independent of all such considerations.

30. There are two great dangers which beset an inexperienced composer of melodies from opposite quarters, which ought not to be passed over in this place. One of these dangers arises from the natural tendency which exists to fall into conventionalisms and hackneyed phrases. Nothing vulgarises a tune so much as this. The other and opposite danger is a certain morbid craving after originality with which many young composers seem to be afflicted. Such a tendency is utterly destructive of all real melody, for it chokes spontaneous origination at its birth. It is impossible too strongly to warn a beginner against these two pitfalls.

31. We have seen that melody ought to be written in a definite and regular scale, that it should begin and end in the same key, that it should be conceived in systematic rhythm, and above all that it should be symmetrical. As a deduction from some of these data, it is clear that those melodies can alone be considered *perfect* which adapt themselves readily to harmony. For a melody which can only be harmonised awkwardly (as for example a large number of so-called Gregorian chants and hymns), however pleasing it may appear to some persons when heard by itself, can yet never produce perfect music. For the strained and unnatural harmonies which are required to accompany such a melody are in themselves a drawback to the excellence of the compound, and forbid us to reckon the music thus produced as perfect. It should be remembered that music consists of two essential elements, melody and harmony. Melody conceived without harmony is the music of barbarous and savage nations, or else of the old days before harmony was discovered. Every musical person now-a-days who has the power of mentally conceiving melody, also conceives (albeit unconsciously) a harmonic accompaniment thereto. In the case of an educated musical ear, the one necessarily involves the other. It is therefore obvious that a melody deprived of the natural harmony which belongs to it, and was conceived with it, only embodies half the original conception, and is therefore imperfect music. On the other hand harmony without melody can never interest a hearer. It can convey no definite emotion to his mind. It has no outline to define it. It has no primary idea to illustrate. It must ever be vague and unsatisfactory, and akin to the mournful sighing of the breeze, as it plays among the strings of an Aeolian harp. It is obvious then that these twin sisters, Melody and Harmony, should never be separated; they cannot thrive apart.

32. The following rules are given in conclusion by way of advice to young composers :—

  i. Never attempt to get rid of the idea of harmony which will always come into your head together with any melody you may conceive.

 ii. Never allow yourself to modulate from key to key on any instrument without an effort to produce some melody along with your harmonies.

iii. Never commit to paper, and retain as approved, any melodic conception which fails to realise all those conditions of perfection which have been enumerated in this chapter.

 iv. Never rest satisfied with any composition, however good may be its harmony, form, counterpoint, or instrumentation, unless it is founded on regular and interesting melodies.

  v. Get into a habit of analysing melodies according to the principles laid down in this chapter. For the better guidance of the student in the work of analysis a few specimens have been given at the end of this volume, pp. 62 to 67, Nos. 1, 2, 3, 4, 5 and 6.

CHAPTER III.

On Form.

1. FORM in music may be defined as "The art of balancing the constituent parts of a composition with reference to symmetry of construction." We have already seen the importance of this principle as applied to a simple melody. But still more important does it become when we are engaged on more extended and complicated works. Of course the selection of forms must be purely arbitrary, and those forms will be best which most perfectly economise new ideas, without involving tedious repetition and prolixity.

2. If a long composition consist of a succession of new ideas strung together without regard to regularity of order, it will be impossible for the hearer to enter into any of them so as to engrave them on his memory; for each succeeding idea will drive away and efface the impression of the last. To avoid this result it is essential that the principal ideas should be introduced more than once, according to some systematic plan.

3. On the other hand, if the principal ideas are too frequently and injudiciously reiterated, the hearer will tire of them before the whole piece is concluded, and thus all interest will be lost. It is the object of *rules of form* to steer clear of these two opposite dangers.

4. There are many kinds of form which have been adopted and commended to us by the best classical composers, of which it will be necessary to treat in order. The principal forms are the following:—

1. The Ancient Binary Form.
2. The Modern Binary Form.
3. The Ternary Form.
4. The Minuet Form.
5. The Rondo Form.
6. The Variations Form.
7. The Fugue Form.

Of these seven species the last, or Fugue Form, has been already sufficiently explained in the author's "Treatise on Counterpoint, Canon, and Fugue," to which the student is referred, and no further explanation of it will be needed in this volume. The other six must be examined separately, together with certain minor varieties, which may be looked upon as derived from some of the above.

5. All these forms are *arbitrary*. It is perfectly conceivable that some great genius—a second Haydn, Mozart, or Beethoven—may invent some new form of equal value. But such geniuses, who can thus revolutionise the whole musical world, are not of frequent occurrence, and it would betoken no small arrogance in an ordinary musical student to attempt such a feat. Equally to be deprecated is that false feeling of independence which sometimes prompts composers to dispense with all regularity of form whatsoever. Of both these pitfalls let the student beware.

CHAPTER IV.

Of the Ancient Binary Form.

1. THIS is probably the oldest species of form, as it is unquestionably derived from ancient dance music, the origin of which is lost in antiquity. It consists, as its name imports, of two parts, the latter of which must be in some way the complement or response to the former. Most old songs are written on this model, and we also find it in Gavottes, Corantos, Rigadoons, Jiggs, and other old-fashioned dance-tunes, such as were used to make up "sets," or "suites de pièces," down to the days of Bach and Handel. We here give two varieties of this form.

No. 1.

i. Principal melody, say sixteen bars, in principal key.

ii. Combining passages modulating simply and quickly into the key of the dominant.

iii. Second melody in dominant key concluding the first division, with or without a "repeat."

F

   iv. Principal melody (No. i.) transposed into key of Dominant, and perhaps curtailed slightly.

   v. Combining passages modulating simply and briefly into original key.

   vi. Second melody transposed into original key, and so concluding the whole piece.

No. 2.

   i. Principal melody in principal key, leading into

   ii. Secondary melody in key of dominant, after which a return to original melody curtailed, concluding in the same with double bar, and a repeat.

   iii. New melody in relative major or minor (as the case may be), treated with secondary melody, &c., exactly like the former division, and ending in the same key as it begins; then Da Capo, the original first division, ending at the first double bar.

2. Most of Handel's songs are written in one or other of the above varieties of this form. Some examples will be found at the end of this Volume.

CHAPTER V.

Of the Modern Binary Form.

1. This is the most important form of all. Every one of the symphonies of Haydn and Mozart, and the earlier ones of Beethoven*, contain movements cast in this mould: and every composer who has followed in their track has given us specimens of it in symphonies, overtures, concertos, sonatas, and chamber-music for stringed instruments; nor are there wanting numerous good instances of it as applied to vocal music also.

2. Like the last-described form, it is divided into two parts, or sections, generally (though not always) separated by a double bar, and often with a repeat.

3. The former division or section contains all the *raw material*, all the original melodies of the piece. These succeed each other without contrapuntal or harmonic developments, according to a certain order of key-sequence.

The order will be as follows if the piece is in a major key :—

    a. First original theme or melody in the principal key; it may be of 8, 12, 16, 20, or 24 bars' length; it may be made according to the rules for melody laid down in Chapter II, § 14–20; and may vary in length and in character according to the dimensions intended for the whole piece.

---

* It might indeed be said that *all* Beethoven's Symphonies contained movements in the Modern Binary Form, if we were to use the term in a somewhat looser sense. For the only essential departure from the regular formula in which the great Composer indulges in these movements is in substituting some other nearly-related key for that of the dominant in the first introduction of the second theme or melody. Still, this *is* an irregularity, though a beautiful one in such hands, and therefore justifies the general assertion in the text.

β. The *Bridge,* composed of modulating passages, to lead from the first to the second theme. These passages may be new, or they may be made out of fragments of the original theme; they may be melodic in character, or not, according to circumstances. They should be so contrived as to lead the ear to expect some new theme in the key of the dominant, and for this purpose they should generally be concluded by some sort of pedal on the *dominant of the new key.* Thus for example, supposing the original theme to be in the key of D major, the bridge should consist of passages or progressions modulating in some such way as the following:—

No. 1.

or, No. 2.

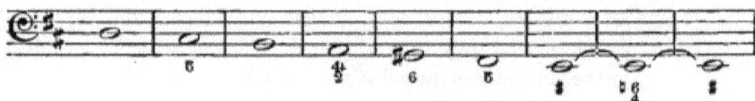

or, No. 3.

or, No. 4.

γ. The bridge leads us into the key of the dominant, on which must now be introduced a second original theme or melody. This should present some points of contrast with the character of the first theme for the sake of variety, and may vary in length according to circumstances.

δ. A few passages of a tolerably brilliant kind should lead to a perfect close in the key of the dominant, thus forming the conclusion of the first section of the piece.

4. In the second section of the composition should be developed the ideas already enunciated in the first part. But it may be divided into two subsections, in the former of which these developments are chiefly put.

a. In fact the only use of this former sub-section is to give an opportunity for the development of ideas. These developments should be of a contrapuntal, canonical, imitative, or fugal kind, and therefore it is often desirable so to construct such original melodies as may work well together in double counterpoint. The student may be referred also to the remarks on fugal *Episodes* in the author's "Treatise on Counterpoint, Canon, and Fugue," Chapter XXII, for various modes of imitative treatment, which may well be introduced in this part of a piece. As to modulation, this subsection ought not to begin in the original key, especially if the first division of the piece has been *repeated*. But it may start in any of the following keys:—

    i. The dominant major;

    ii. The dominant minor;

    iii. The supertonic major;
    iv. The mediant minor;
     v. The tonic minor;
    vi. The minor-mediant major.

The modulations employed may be left to the un-fettered fancy of the composer, provided only they never transgress the rules of harmony, or the dictates of good taste. The length of this subsection is very various according to circumstances. If the original ideas do not lend themselves sufficiently well to development, it is allowable to introduce a new original idea contrived expressly to work in with those already existing. This subsection ought to end with the harmony of the dominant of the original key, intensifying its dominant character, if need be, by the introduction of a dominant pedal leading directly into the second subsection.

β. This second subsection may be looked upon as the dénoûment of the whole piece. It usually begins by repeating the original theme or melody in the original key, either exactly or with such variations and curtailments as the case may seem to demand. This is followed by a bridge of modulating passages analogous to, but yet different from, that in the former division. In the present case it should lead first from, and then back to the original key, introducing it, if necessary, with a dominant pedal. After this comes the second original theme in the key of the tonic, (and not as before in that of the dominant,) and thus with a few brilliant passages, and concluding chords, the whole piece comes to a satisfactory termination.

If the composer wishes to lengthen the piece he may do it in many ways. Accessory passages may be added to either or both of the principal themes; or the developments of the former subsection may be extended into real episodes; or a coda may be added at the end, which may either consist of brilliant passages, or may itself be an episode, or may be formed of fugal developments analogous to those described above.

If it be desired, on the other hand, to shorten the piece, the former subsection containing the developments may be curtailed, or even almost omitted, as is generally done in the overtures of Italian operas, and in the first movements of short easy sonatines.

5. If the piece be in the minor key the order will be as follows:

FIRST DIVISION.

α. First original theme in original key.

β. Bridge modulating into relative major, and ending generally with a dominant pedal in that key, so as to lead the ear to expect the

γ. Second principal theme, in the key of the relative major.

δ. Accessory passages, &c., concluding this division in the key of the relative major.

SECOND DIVISION.

α. First subsection. Developments, beginning in one of the following keys:

  i. Relative major;

  ii. Minor of relative key;

iii. Key of minor seventh, major;

iv. Submediant-major;

v. Submediant-minor;

vi. Flattened tonic major:

it will then modulate contrapuntally or otherwise as above
described, and so lead (by a dominant pedal generally)
into the

β. Second subsection, which commences with the original theme
in the original key, and is conducted exactly like a piece
in the major key, as above described, except that

γ. The second principal theme may be reproduced either in the
minor or the major of the original key. This will of
course depend partly on the character of the melody, and
partly on the taste of the composer. If brilliancy and
strong contrast are required, it will be best to conclude
in the major. If the whole piece is intended to partake
of a pathetic or mysterious character, then a minor
conclusion will be preferred.

δ. It may be observed that sometimes, though rarely, the second
principal subject is introduced into the first division in the
minor key of the dominant, instead of the relative major,
that division therefore ending in a minor key. In such
a case it is obvious that the modulations in the second
division will have to be somewhat modified.

6. We will now give a general tabular view of the binary form, to
assist the student in impressing it on his memory.

FIRST DIVISION.

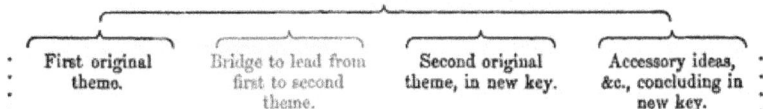

First original theme.	Bridge to lead from first to second theme.	Second original theme, in new key.	Accessory ideas, &c., concluding in new key.

SECOND DIVISION.

First Subsection.

Perpetual modulations and developments.	Half close on dominant (pedal) of original key.

Second Subsection.

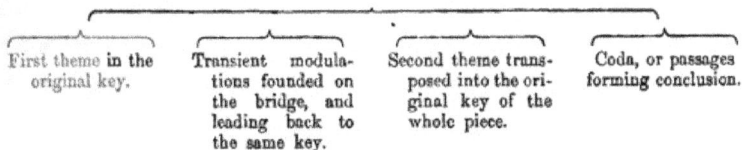

First theme in the original key.	Transient modulations founded on the bridge, and leading back to the same key.	Second theme transposed into the original key of the whole piece.	Coda, or passages forming conclusion.

G

CHAPTER VI.

Of the Ternary Form.

1. This form divides a piece into three portions of about equal length.

2. The first portion is devoted to the exposition of the original melodies or themes on which the whole piece is to be built. It should begin and end in the same key, and only transient modulations and short developments are admissible.

3. The second portion is formed like the first. It must however begin and end in some different key from the preceding. It must be also the exponent of new themes. Only transient modulations and short developments can be admitted. It should end in the key in which it begins. Its length should be, as nearly as may be, the same as that of the first portion. The key in which it is composed should be nearly related to that of the first portion, so as to succeed it without the intervention of modulating chords or passages. The parts are separated by a double bar, generally without "repeats."

4. The third portion generally begins in the original key of the piece, in which of course it also concludes. No new theme should be here introduced. Modulations are admissible and desirable, provided the original key be never entirely forgotten. Developments of the themes contained in both the preceding portions should form the principal material used, and the whole should culminate in a brilliant and effective coda formed in a similar way.

5. We subjoin a tabular view of this form.

FIRST PORTION.	SECOND PORTION.	THIRD PORTION.
Exposition of themes; hardly any modulation or development; end in original key.	Commence and end in some nearly-related key; new themes, treated as in first portion in all respects.	Modulating developments formed out of all previous themes, beginning and ending in original key, and concluding with coda.

CHAPTER VII.

Of the Minuet Form.

1. THIS is a light and pleasing form, of smaller dimensions than the foregoing, it is useful as a contrast or relief between two longer movements in a graver style.

2. The original minuet form always consisted of a piece in triple time and of moderate speed, to which was attached a "trio" or additional movement, always ending with a repetition of the minuet itself.

3. The minuet and trio were always written in the short or ancient binary form, No. 1 *, each consisting of two portions separated by a double bar, and each portion repeated; excepting when the minuet was played over for the last time after the trio, when no repeats were made.   To ensure this, at the end of the trio the words "Menuetto Da Capo senza replica" were usually inserted.   The trio was almost always in some nearly related key.

4. Sometimes a few additional bars by way of coda were added to the minuet after its last repetition, with the object of leading smoothly into the succeeding movement.

An example of a regular minuet and trio will be found at pp. 123 to 127.

* Vide p. 33.

5. Beethoven introduced a more lively style of minuet and trio, called a scherzo. A regular scherzo exactly resembles a minuet and trio, save that it is generally in $\frac{3}{8}$ time, and is always much quicker and more lively than the older form.

6. Sometimes the trio of a scherzo is not a distinct movement, but is rather a mere prolongation of the scherzo, dispensing with the usual repeats.

7. Lastly Beethoven and after him Mendelssohn and others substituted a movement in $\frac{2}{4}$ time for the scherzo, or for the trio, or for both. Such a movement often assumes larger dimensions, and is written in the modern binary form. In such a case it is called an "Intermezzo."

8. Any of the foregoing modifications of the regular minuet may be advantageously adopted according to the requirements of the piece into which they are to be introduced.

9. If it is desired to lengthen a regular minuet, a second or even a third trio may be added, always provided that the minuet, without repeats, be played again between each trio, and at the end of the whole.

10. If the minuet form is adopted for a complete and isolated composition, it should be lengthened considerably, and then both the minuet and trio may be written in the ternary form.

11. Marches are written mostly in the minuet form, only in common time, and with a frequent use of the peculiar march-rhythm

. They generally have more than one trio, and very often also a brilliant coda to conclude.

12. One peculiar variety of march exists, which Meyerbeer has in a great measure made his own, called a Torch-March, Marche aux

Flambeaux, or (with more accuracy) Fakeltanz; which is rather a
minuet than a march, and is played by a military band at grand
Royal Weddings in Prussia, Bavaria, and a few other German Courts.
Although very military in general style, it is written in very slow
triple time, which invests it with a pompous and courtly character
more akin to the old "Minuet de la Cour" than to anything else. It
is of considerable length, and contains several trios and episodes, besides
a coda to conclude.

CHAPTER VIII.

Of the Rondo Form.

1. THIS form is of two kinds, one developed out of the Binary, and the other out of the Ternary Form.

2. Its chief characteristic in every case is the continual recurrence of the first original theme, with which every division and sub-section must always conclude, save that at the last repetition it may be followed by a final coda.

3. Every repercussion of the original theme must be in its own original key. But certain curtailments or variations of it may be admitted when its repetitions are many.

4. As it follows from the reappearance of the original theme at every double bar that each division and sub-section will end in the original key, certain modifications of the modulations and successions of key will be necessitated, which will be sufficiently obvious to the student without being minutely described here.

5. As the original theme will be very often heard during the course of the piece, it will be best to avoid making it more than sixteen bars in length, although accessory melodies may be appended to it on its first appearance, which may advantageously be omitted afterwards. The second original theme may be made of longer dimensions, as it will only be heard twice during the course of the piece, and then in different keys.

6. We will now give a tabular view of the Rondo Form, which will sufficiently explain its structure.

FIRST RONDO FORM, DERIVED FROM BINARY FORM.

FIRST DIVISION.

First original theme, with accessory melodies, &c., often ending with theme repeated.	Bridge to lead from first to second theme.	Second original theme, in new key.	Accessory ideas and passages modulating back to	First theme, curtailed and repeated in its original key.

SECOND DIVISION.

FIRST SUBSECTION.

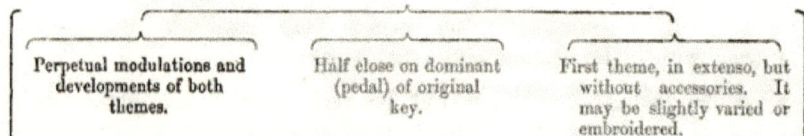

Perpetual modulations and developments of both themes.	Half close on dominant (pedal) of original key.	First theme, in extenso, but without accessories. It may be slightly varied or embroidered.

SECOND SUBSECTION.

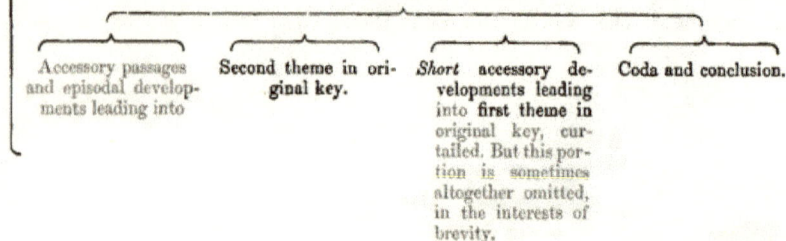

Accessory passages and episodal developments leading into	Second theme in original key.	Short accessory developments leading into first theme in original key, curtailed. But this portion is sometimes altogether omitted, in the interests of brevity.	Coda and conclusion.

SECOND RONDO FORM, DERIVED FROM TERNARY FORM.

FIRST PORTION.

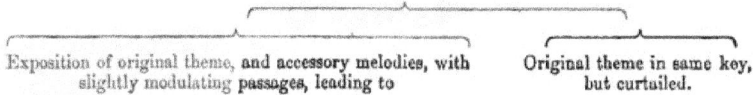

Exposition of original theme, and accessory melodies, with slightly modulating passages, leading to	Original theme in same key, but curtailed.

SECOND PORTION.

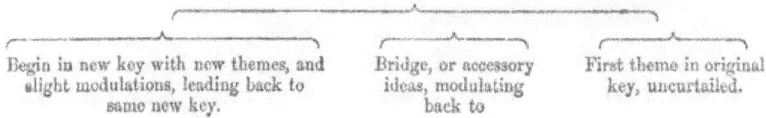

Begin in new key with new themes, and slight modulations, leading back to same new key.	Bridge, or accessory ideas, modulating back to	First theme in original key, uncurtailed.

THIRD PORTION.

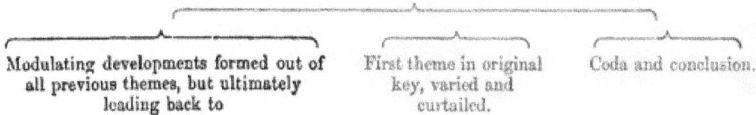

Modulating developments formed out of all previous themes, but ultimately leading back to	First theme in original key, varied and curtailed.	Coda and conclusion.

CHAPTER IX.

Of the Air with Variations.

1. This form is used either for complete isolated pieces, or as part of more extended compositions.

2. It is perhaps one of the oldest forms, as it was very commonly employed three hundred years ago for virginal music, and "consorts for viols." It almost always formed part of regular suites de pièces for the spinet and harpsichord, down to the time of J. S. Bach and Handel*. It was often introduced into symphonies, quartetts, and sonatas, by Haydn, Mozart, Beethoven, and their followers. Lastly, a very florid and brilliant form of it has been used in the composition of a large quantity of modern pianoforte music. It is therefore on the whole

---

* There is a considerable analogy between this form and the ancient custom of writing "Divisions upon a Ground Bass." Admirable specimens of movements thus contrived may be found in the works of Purcell, Blow, and other English composers of the latter part of the seventeenth century. Also in those of Handel and J. Sebastian Bach. The "Ground Bass" (in Italian "Basso ostinato") is a short series of notes, repeated over and over again continuously throughout the whole movement, over which as many various melodies and harmonies are placed as can be made to agree with it. Generally the ground bass is entirely confined to the key of the piece; but occasionally it is allowed to change to some nearly related key. As an example of a ground bass in one invariable key, I would quote the beautiful song, "When I am laid in earth," in Purcell's "Dido and Æneas"; while as an instance of a ground bass which is allowed to modulate I would refer to the chorus "To song and dance," in Handel's oratorio of "Samson."

a form of considerable importance, although perhaps inferior from an artistic point of view to those we have already described.

3. Variations may be constructed either upon an original theme or motivo, or upon some well-known or popular melody. The latter is the plan commonly adopted by modern composers of pianoforte music. The former is the more classical way, and ought alone to be used when a theme with variations forms a part of a larger work. The two ways however are of equal antiquity, and have both been adopted by some of the best ancient and modern composers of instrumental music.

4. The character of the variations will vary according to that of the instrument, or combination of instruments, for which they are intended. And therefore the rules we shall here give must be subject to many corresponding modifications according to circumstances.

5. The following are some of the ways in which melodies may be varied:

    i. Preserve the melody unaltered, but vary the accompaniments by introducing more florid figures and rapid passages.

    ii. Ornament the melody with grace-notes, shakes, appoggiaturas, passing and auxiliary notes, turns, and the like.

    iii. Introduce brilliant passages continuously which shall contain in them the notes of the melody, while at the same time they form an embroidery thereon.

    iv. Put the melody, if major, into the minor of the key, or into the relative minor; or, if it be minor, then into a major key; so as to alter its character.

    v. Change the pace of the melody from fast to slow, or from slow to fast; or else change the time of it from common to triple, or from simple to compound, or the converse of these.

vi. Put the melody in the bass, or in an inner part, and weave in a new melody with it in the upper part.

vii. Treat the theme canonically, or with perpetual imitations, and various counterpoints.

viii. Combine some of the above ways together if the theme will admit of it.

6. There is of course no rule which limits the number of variations which may be successively introduced, except the requirements of good taste. Suffice it to say that if they exceed a certain limit extreme weariness is sure to be produced.

CHAPTER X.

Of the Fugue Form.

1. For a detailed account of this form the student is referred to the author's " Treatise on Counterpoint, Canon, and Fugue," where the subject is fully discussed.

2. But the fugue form may be combined with the modern binary form very advantageously, either in overtures or in the last movements of sonatas, symphonies, and quartetts. Perhaps the finest examples of such a combination are the overture to Mozart's opera " Die Zauberflöte," and the finale to his symphony in C, No. 6. We specially recommend the student to examine and analyse these magnificent works, and to imitate them as far as he can.

3. A fugue on the original theme will often make a good finale to a set of variations.

CHAPTER XI.

Of Combinations of Forms.

1. THE various forms described in the preceding chapters are often grouped together to constitute the different "movements," of which the larger sort of instrumental works consist.

2. Thus are constructed symphonies and sonatas; string-trios, quartetts, quintetts, sestetts, septetts, and ottetts; overtures and concertos; and also, sometimes, though much more rarely, certain vocal compositions.

3. A symphony is by far the most important composition of all, as regards the powers and resources of *absolute music,* i.e. music which depends solely on itself for its effects, and is in no wise dependent on words, scenery, acting, or any other extraneous condition. Therefore a symphony may be regarded as the highest development to which the art of music has ever attained.

4. A symphony is a work composed for a full orchestra; it consists of three or four distinct movements, each movement being complete in itself; and involves all the known resources of pure musical art.

5. The first movement of a symphony is usually an allegro, a tolerably brisk piece (preceded sometimes, however, by an introduction

in slow time, in no particular form, of a majestic or mysterious character). This allegro is almost always written in the regular modern binary form, as described in Chapter V.

6. The second movement of a symphony is generally slow; adagio, largo, or andante. It should be of a deeply impassioned and emotional character, containing good flowing melodies, and striking harmonies. The form may be either modern binary or ternary. Sometimes indeed a theme with variations is substituted, but this is not so common, nor is it a desirable plan to follow. The second movement ought not to be in the same key as the first, but in some nearly related key, so as to avoid monotony, and secure contrast and relief.

7. The third movement should be a minuet and trio, a scherzo, or perhaps an intermezzo. Sometimes this movement is placed before the slow movement, their order being thus inverted. Sometimes it is altogether omitted. In this case again there should be a change of key, care being taken to choose one which will equally well follow what precedes, and lead into that which is to come after.

8. The last, or concluding movement, usually called the finale, should always be in the same key as the first movement, excepting only that when the symphony begins in a minor key, the finale may be either in the minor or the major of the same. This last movement should be generally of a lively and busy character, and should always conclude with a brilliant coda. It may be either in the modern binary, ternary, or rondo form, of which however the last is preferable.

9. The effect of a symphony depends of course, in a very great degree, upon the skill displayed in its instrumentation, of which this

is not the place to speak. Every student who has an ambition to try this highest walk of art, must carefully study the theory and practice of writing for various instruments, and devote much time and pains to the analysis of the symphonies of Haydn, Mozart, Beethoven, Spohr, and Mendelssohn.

10. A sonata is a work composed for one, or at the most for two instruments; generally for the pianoforte. As regards its form however it is identical with the symphony, and therefore all the rules for the composition of symphonies in that respect will equally apply to the case of sonatas.

11. If it is desired to write a very short sonata, the developments of the binary movements must be curtailed, and the third movement omitted. The composition will then be properly called a *Sonatina*.

12. The modern binary form is often but inaccurately styled "the sonata form," on account of its being always adopted for the principal movements of sonatas.

13. The term sonata was also formerly applied to short concerted pieces for three or four stringed instruments, as in the case of those by Corelli, Geminiani, and Purcell. But this application of the word has long since fallen into disuse.

14. Chamber-music is the name given to trios, quartetts, quintetts, sestetts, septetts, and ottetts, for instruments of the violin class, or for these in conjunction with the pianoforte. All such compositions are written on the same model as symphonies and sonatas, as far as form is concerned. Sometimes also compositions of exactly similar form and kind are written for various wind instruments, with or without the pianoforte; or for a combination of wind and stringed instruments. These however are not so common at present as they ought to be,

considering the marvellous variety of beautiful effects which they can produce. In all these cases it should be borne in mind that they differ from symphonies by having one instrument only to each part.

15. Concertos are symphonies in which some one instrument (or at most two instruments) bear a prominent part, the rest of the orchestra being only employed to support them either by accompaniment, alternation, or contrast. In form concertos differ in no essential respect from the foregoing kinds of composition. It will therefore be needless to enlarge on them further.

16. Overtures are either instrumental movements prefixed to oratorios and operas, or independent compositions for the orchestra, in which latter case they are properly styled Concert Overtures. They are almost invariably written in the modern binary form, only with the second section curtailed more or less, especially in its first sub-section (see page 37). Before the time of Haydn, overtures consisted of three movements, or more rarely of two. The first was a pompous sort of slow introduction, the second a quick fugal movement, and the third a minuet or a march. Mozart revived the fugal movement in his grand overture to "Die Zauberflöte," combining it most wonderfully with the modern binary form. It is to be regretted that this admirable compound form of overture has not been more extensively adopted.

CHAPTER XII.

Of Vocal Composition.

1. It has already been observed that regular form is mainly applicable to instrumental music rather than to vocal; and the reason is this, — that in vocal music the first consideration must always be the words to which it is set. Still, for all that, there are many cases in which vocal music may also be advantageously cast in a regular form, without any detriment to the words. Whenever this is the case, it is very desirable to avail oneself of the facility thus afforded.

2. Many slight songs and duets for voices with accompaniment for the pianoforte are set to such very weak and almost unmeaning words that these may count for almost nothing, and the music must as it were shine by its own intrinsic light. It will be a great advantage then to let it assume some regular form. The best will generally be either of the kinds of ancient binary, or the modern binary curtailed and simplified. An example of such vocal music, which is deserving of careful study, may be found in Haydn's celebrated canzonets. Most of Handel's songs are likewise set in the ancient binary form. Mozart also frequently writes his airs in the modern binary form. Nor are examples of the ternary form by any means wanting. There are other cases again in which the words themselves are suggestive of some

regular form. When this is the case, it ought of course to be unhesitatingly adopted.

3. But the fugue form is perhaps the commonest of all in the case of sacred choruses, and it should be freely adopted whenever it does not too much obscure the sense of the words.

4. National songs and choruses often take the form of a kind of vocal march, and should be considered as specimens of ancient binary form.

5. Hymn tunes are very regular in form, but their form is merely the short binary form of a regular melody, as described in the second chapter of this work.

6. Anthems are often nearly formless, and simply follow the rhythm of the words to which they are set. But frequently they contain movements in the fugue form, and also, in the case of many more recent specimens, there are movements in a curtailed modern binary form. For example, that fine anthem by Sir John Goss, "If we believe that Jesus died," and the second movement of his "Praise the Lord, O my soul."

7. Many of the motetts of Haydn and Mozart are written strictly in the modern binary form; for example, Haydn's "Insanae et vanae curae," and Mozart's "Splendente Te Deus." And again, in his "Misericordias Domini," Mozart has combined the binary and fugue forms in a masterly way. All these specimens, and many more like them, should be carefully studied by the young composer.

8. There is another form, almost exclusively vocal, which ought not to be passed over here. This is the round, or free canon. In this, one voice begins a melody and completes one division of it. Then

another voice sings the same, while the former voice continues the
next division of it, which must be so constructed as to run in correct
double counterpoint with it. Then a third voice comes in under the
same conditions, and so forth. This is an exceedingly pleasing kind of
composition, and much to be recommended. The late Sir Henry R.
Bishop greatly excelled in this style of music. His "When the wind
blows," "Hark! 'tis the Indian drum," "To see his face," and many
others, deserve to live in the memory of more than one generation.
Cherubini was also a master in the art of composing such pieces. His
"Perfida Clori" is too well known and admired to need further praise
here. The student may be also referred to such examples as Rossini's
"Cielo il mio labbro ispira," Curschman's "Ti prego, O madre pia," and
Leslie's "O memory."

9. When the round or free canon is wedded to comic or humorous
words, the piece is called a "catch," and the aim of the composer
should be to interweave the parts in such a manner as shall best
illustrate and bring out the amusing ideas intended to be conveyed
by the words. As examples may be named Dr. Nares' "Wilt thou
lend me thy mare;" J. Baildon's "Mister Speaker, though 'tis late;"
S. Webbe's "Would you know my Celia's charms;" and Dr. Callcott's
"Ah! how, Sophia."

CHAPTER XIII.

1. THERE are many compositions which cannot be brought under any of the foregoing heads, and which yet possess a certain regularity of structure peculiar to themselves. Some writers would class all these works together, as composed in the "Coupe de Fantaisie," or fantasia form. But it is better perhaps to regard them as individual attempts to invent new forms, each of which might be followed by other composers, did it seem equally applicable to any but the one composition in which it first appeared. For, after all, regular forms are absolutely arbitrary, and are recognised and recommended chiefly because experience, and the practice of the best composers, have demonstrated their superior excellence and value.

2. The great danger of going in search of new forms, lies in the risk of losing all regularity of structure, and thus destroying every advantage which a regular form could supply. The young composer is therefore advised on no account to attempt new forms, especially in instrumental music, but to be content with getting as many original effects as he can out of the old forms. A first-class composer of long experience may of course do with impunity what would be an act of conceited folly in a tyro, and matured genius may earn praise for judiciously violating rules, the infraction of which would justly expose a younger composer to ridicule and censure. Therefore an example of daring license from the approved works of a classical writer ought never

to be adduced as an excuse for errors in the music of a learner. It is always necessary to acquire the habit of observing rules with facility before beginning to seek ways and means of breaking them.

3. But above all should the composer's motto be "Ars celare artem." In other words, let him strive to introduce all the resources of the art, whether of harmony, counterpoint, form, or instrumentation, without letting the labour of such devices appear conspicuously in his compositions. All should be done naturally, easily, and as it were spontaneously, otherwise half the effect of the science employed will be entirely neutralised.

4. Prolixity, again, should be carefully avoided. It is far better for the audience to wish for more, and call for a repetition of the piece, than for them to be wearied with it, and wish it over before its conclusion.

5. There is sometimes a tendency among modern composers to make melody and regularity of design altogether subsidiary to instrumental effect. Such a method of proceeding is greatly to be deprecated, inasmuch as it is a complete inversion of the true order of things. The better way is always to begin with the melody, then harmonise it, then extend it and continue it with other melodies according to some regular form, then introduce, if need be, the setting off of instrumental variety of effect. For it is herein analogous to the art of painting, where the artist begins with a sketch or out-line, then shades it and gives it substance, then extends and combines together the main features of his picture according to the rules of perspective, and lastly colours the whole, and thus crowns his work. At the same time the general effect of the picture, or of the musical composition, as the case may be, may be conceived

in the mind of the artist, or composer, before he enters on his work. Only when he proceeds to embody his preconceived ideas, he must set about his task *secundum artem*, or else a failure will probably ensue. An orator must be sure that he knows what he wants to say before he begins to speak, or he will speak nonsense, while at the same time he must speak good grammar, and pronounce his words clearly, or he will be unintelligible.

6. We have now gone through the various matters needed to enable the student to acquire the art of composition ; all that remains is to commend the following examples to his careful study, and to express, in conclusion, an earnest hope that this work may help towards the improvement of musical composition and musical criticism in this country.

EXAMPLES.

No. 1.—*A regular Melody by* HAYDN.

By the brackets it will be perceived that this melody consists of two similar and corresponding periods of eight bars each.

Each period is divided into two phrases of four bars each.

Each phrase is made up of two strains of two bars each.

The first phrase ends with an imperfect cadence on the fifth of the dominant, on the down-beat.

The second phrase concludes with the third of the tonic, but at the up-beat.

The third phrase suggests first a transition into B minor, and then finishes with the third of the dominant on the up-beat.

The fourth phrase winds up the melody with a perfect tonic cadence. This melody is therefore in all respects perfectly regular.

No. 2.—*The " Old Hundredth" tune (equal notes version).*

This tune is perfectly regular. It cannot be subdivided into strains, but consists of two periods of eight bars each, these being subdivided into phrases of four bars.

The only imperfection is the perfect tonic close at the end of the third phrase: were the tune harmonised it would be well to accompany this close with either an inverted chord of G, or with the chord of E minor.

No. 3.—*Melody by* MOZART.

As it stands, this is a perfectly regular period. It can be prolonged by the addition of two bars, partaking of the nature of an echo; thus—

No. 4.—*Melody by* MOZART, *with a similar prolongation.*

No. 5.—*Melody by* HAYDN, *analysed.*

This melody is divided into three periods, of which the first and last are perfectly regular. These each consist of two phrases, and these are subdivided into strains of two bars each.

But the second period is irregular, inasmuch as it contains only six bars, and cannot be split up into phrases, but only into three equal

strains, each of two bars.   It will perhaps be best to look upon the
third of these strains as a kind of interpolated coda, to give emphasis
to the two preceding ones.

This melody affords a good example of *half-bar rhythm*, that is to
say, rhythm commencing always at the latter half of a bar.   When a
melody is so constructed, it is important that this system of rhythm
should be consistently adhered to throughout the whole piece.

No. 6.—*Longer melody, with words, by* DELLA MARIA, *analysed.*

Andante.

(Instrumental ritornello.)

Lorsque dans   une   tour ob - scure   ce jeune homme est dans la   dou -

- leur, Mon cœur gui - dé par la   na - ture   doit com - pa - tir à   son   mal -

- heur.   (Instrumental ritornello.)   Si   j'en - tends sa   plainte   tou -

- chante je deviens triste tout le jour, Ma-man, ne sois pas mécon -

- tente, la pi - tié n'est pas de l'a - mour, la - - pi - tié n'est pas de l'a-mour.

This air is another instance of a melody beginning every strain on the latter half of the bar.

After an instrumental phrase of four bars, divided into two equal strains, the voice begins a period of eight bars, divided into two phrases of four bars, and these again subdivided into strains of two bars each.

Then two bars of instrumental ritornello are interpolated by way of prolongation. The voice then enters upon the second period, which is not so regular as the former one, as its second phrase is lengthened by a coda of two bars, added in order to emphasise the concluding words, these being as it were the pith of the whole sentiment. These irregularities do not in the least impair the symmetrical beauty of the whole air.

No. 7.—*Example of a part of a Duett, in which the parts overlap, so as to apparently cut off the ends of phrases.*

From MARCELLO's Psalms. Psalm vi. 1.

Si - - gnor   quando ar-de il   fuo - co   del -

Si - - - -

1   2   3   4   5   6

- - gius-to Tu - o fu - ro - - - re,   del - gius-to

- gnor   quando ar-de il fuo - co del - gius-to Tu - o fu -

7   8   9   10   11

In the foregoing example the first two bars are an instrumental symphony of one strain. The melody begins at the third bar, with a phrase of four bars divided into two equal strains. Before this phrase is concluded, the second voice enters with a similar melody at the sixth bar, thus apparently, though not really, cutting off the phrase begun by the first voice. At the fifteenth bar the same thing occurs, except that in this case it is the lower voice which leads.

No. 8.—*Analysis of Handel's Air in the Messiah, "But Thou didst not leave."*

The music of this example is not given here, because every one may be supposed to possess a copy of so popular a work as that in which it occurs.

This song is a very good specimen of the ancient binary form. It is in the key of A major, and commences with an orchestral symphony of five bars. The voice then begins the melody at bar 6, which forms a phrase of *five* bars, in consequence of an interpolated bar like an instrumental ritornello. Then follows, at bar 11, a modulation into the key of the dominant, E major, leading to a concluding phrase of melody which closes the first division of the song in the key of E at bar 17.

At bar 18 the first melody is transposed into E, and slightly altered so as to glide into the key of A again at bar 20, in which key the remainder of the air is kept, concluding with an almost exact counterpart of the phrase which ended the former division, only transposed into the key of A, in which the air regularly ends.

––––––––––

Most of Handel's longer airs are written in the second variety of the ancient binary form, of which a specimen will be given hereafter.

Meanwhile it will be well to study the following example of an instrumental piece by the same great composer, in which the bars have been numbered in order to facilitate analysis.

No. 9.—*Gigue from the first "Suite de Pièces," by* HANDEL.

Although there is not much regular **melody** in this piece, **yet it is** a fair example of the **first** variety of the old binary form. The first subject occupies six bars, and is in a quasi-fugal style. At the tenth bar there is a modulation into the key of the dominant, **E**, after which a series of passages lead to a concluding phrase of four bars ending in **E,** at bar **22.**

At bar **23** the first subject is transposed into the key of **E,** and slightly curtailed.

At bar **27** begin a series of modulations to lead back gradually to the key of **A.**

At bar **32** commences a number of passages in the key of **A,** almost identical with those which occurred in the former part in the key of **E.**

The four **concluding bars** correspond with those which closed the former part, only of course transposed into A.

1   2

L

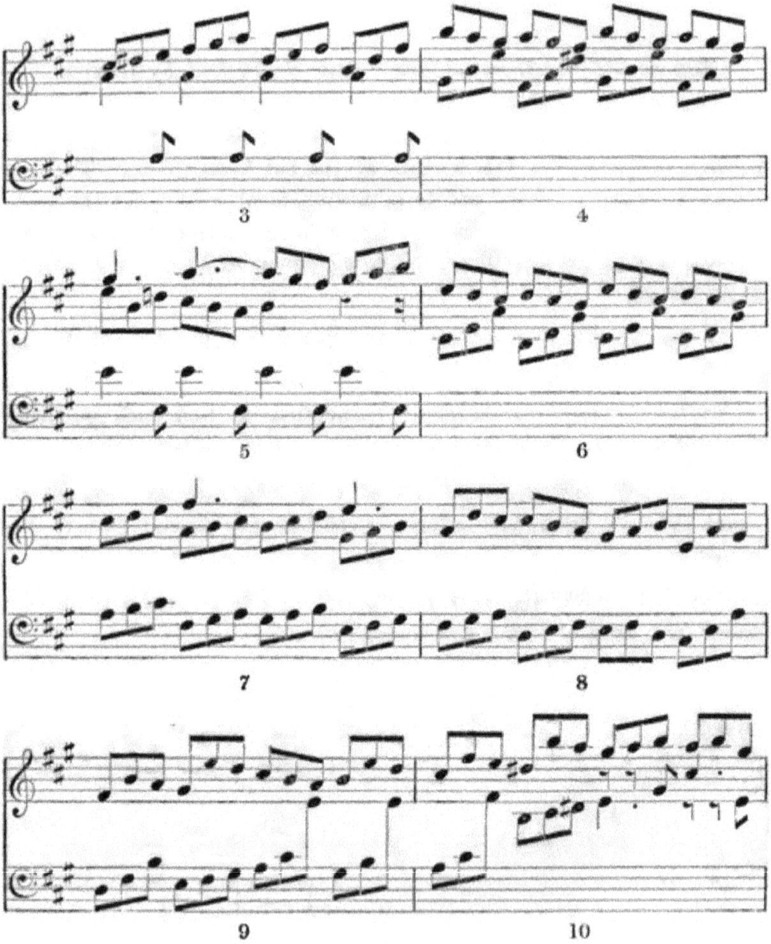
3
4
5
6
7
8
9
10

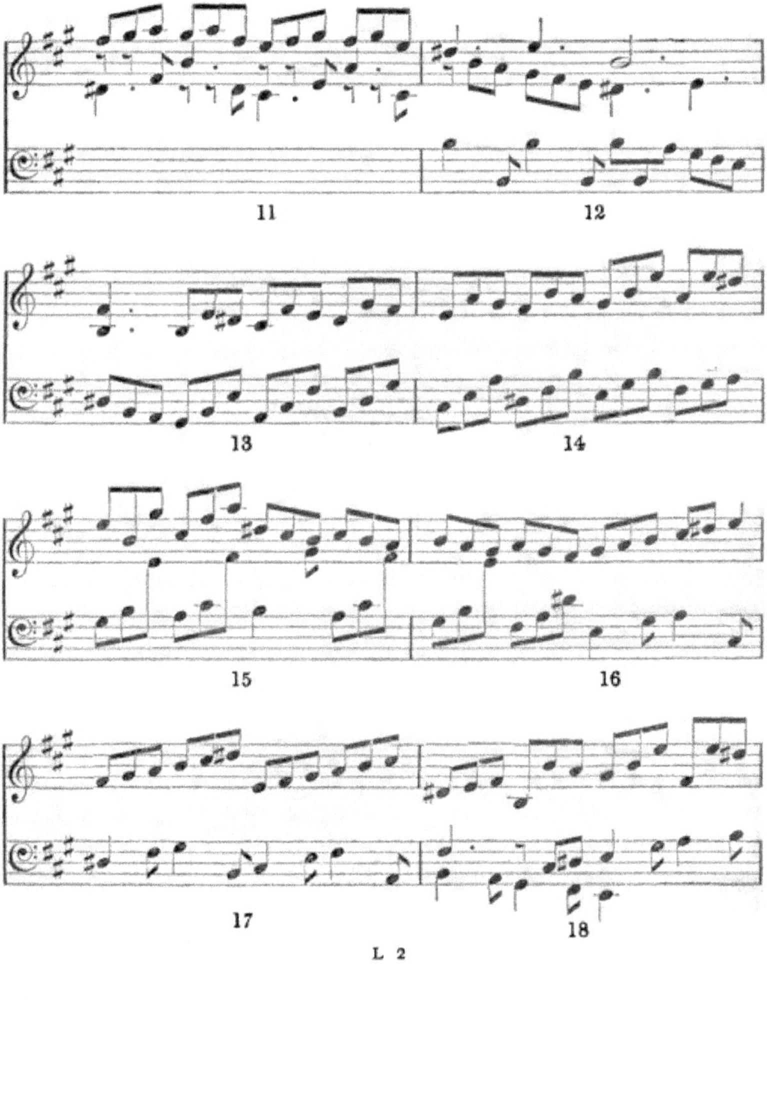
11
12
13
14
15
16
17
18

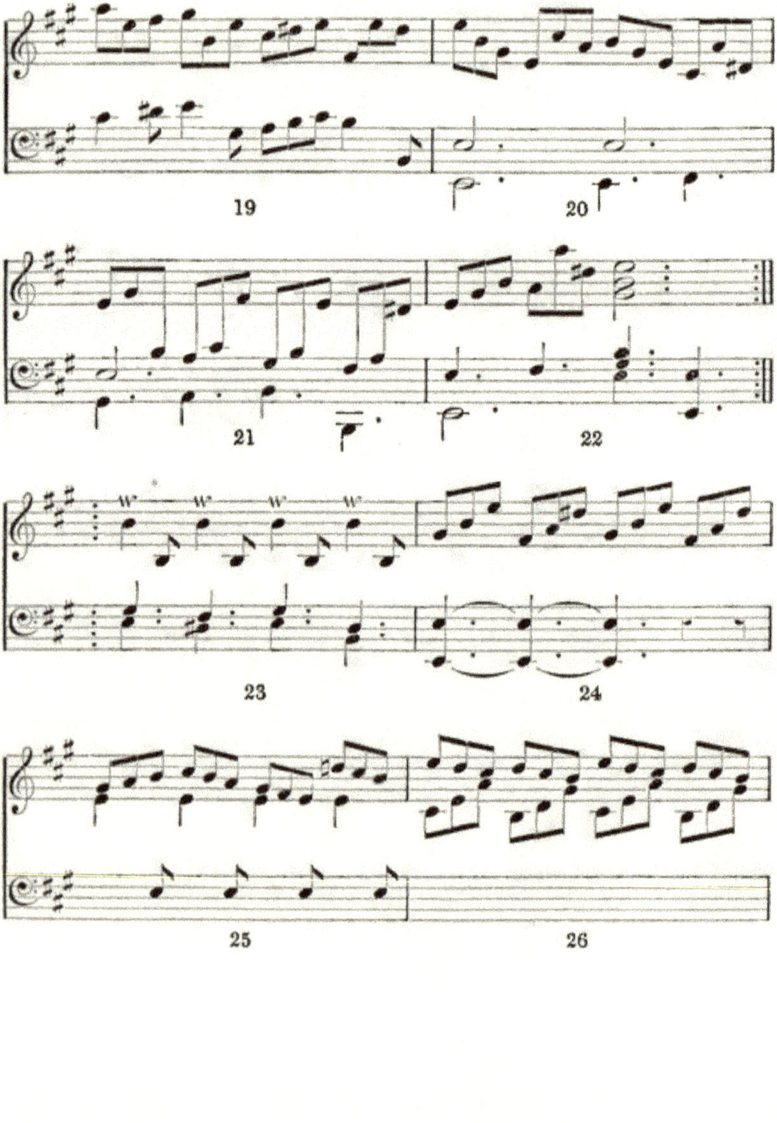
19
20
21
22
23
24
25
26

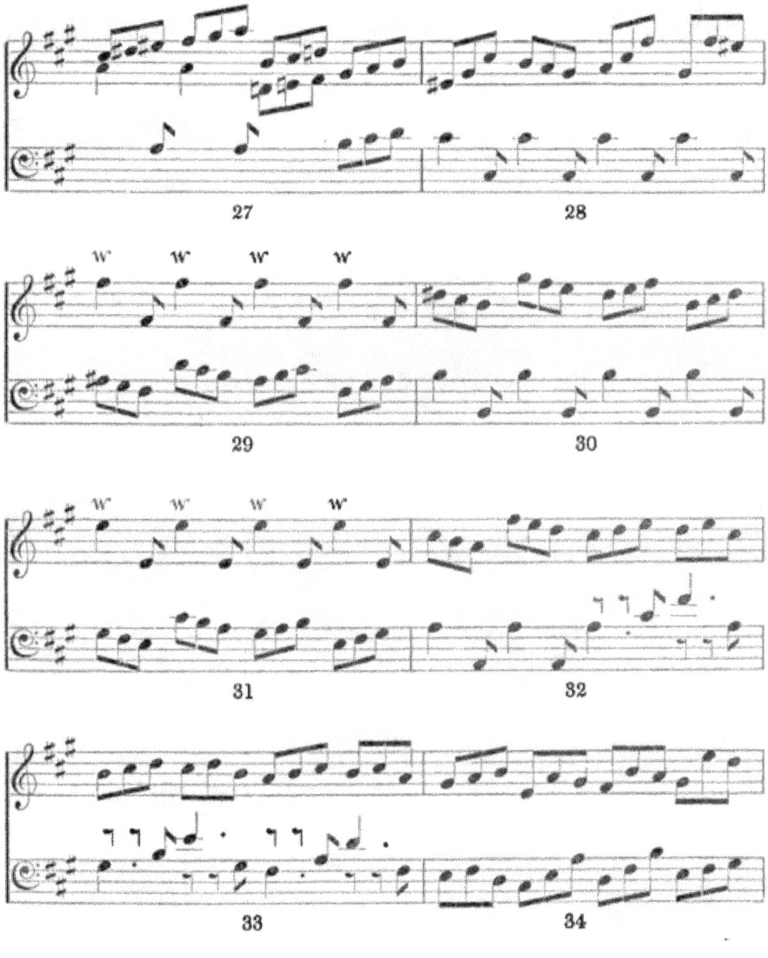
27
28
W W W W
29
30
W W W W
31
32
33
34

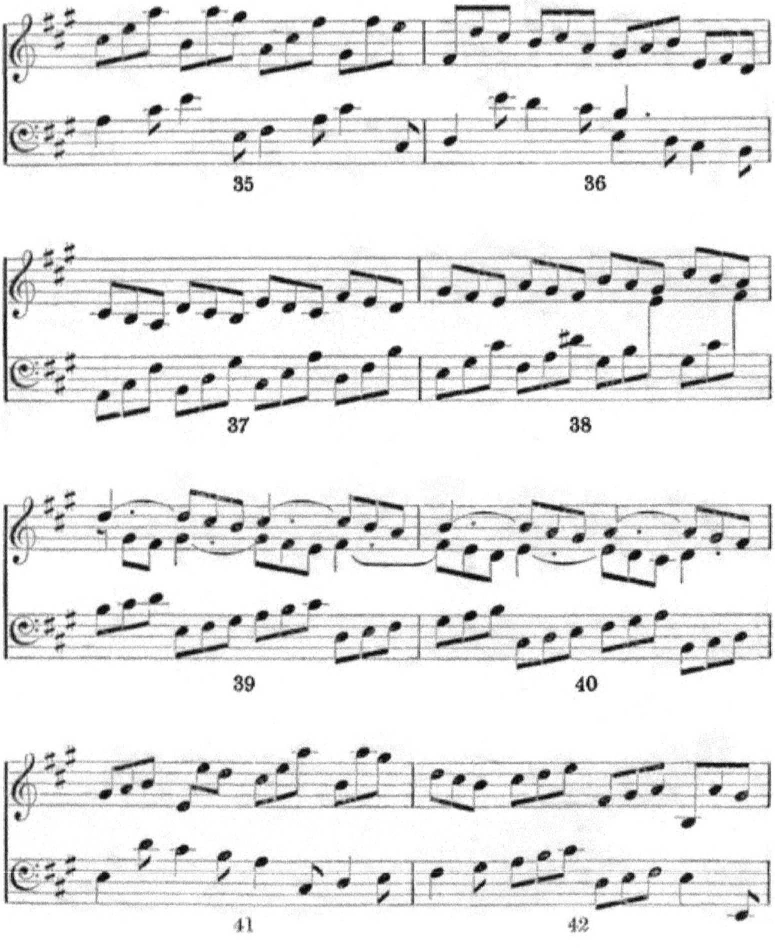
35
36
37
38
39
40
41
42

43   44   45

No. 10.—*Example of First Variety of the Old Binary Form.*

The first twenty-one bars are an instrumental symphony to introduce the voice.

At the 22nd bar the voice enters with the principal melody in the key of A major. This melody is a curiously constructed one, as it is composed of four phrases of *three* bars each.

At the 34th bar the second subject is introduced in the key of E. A short symphony of six bars introduces the first subject transposed into E, and curtailed, so as to return to the original key of A. After which accessory passages lead to the second subject, which reappears at the 73rd bar, transposed into A, in which key the movement concludes.

This air may be regarded as a link between the two varieties of the old binary form, as it possesses a second part, commencing at bar

92, and leading back to a repetition of the original air, 'Dal segno al fine.'

Se spunta amica stella.

Air from the Opera of "Tigrane," by Hasse.

Se spun - ta a -

M

- - mi - ca stel - la, Al ti - mi - do noc - chie - ro,

23   24   25   26   27

Sem - bra ri - den - te e bel - la, Per - chè nel suo sen -

28   29   30   31   32

- - tie - ro, La cal - - - - - - - - -

33   34   35   36   37   38

- - ma . . può - spe - rar, . . . può - spe - rar.

cres.

39   40   41   42   43

M 2

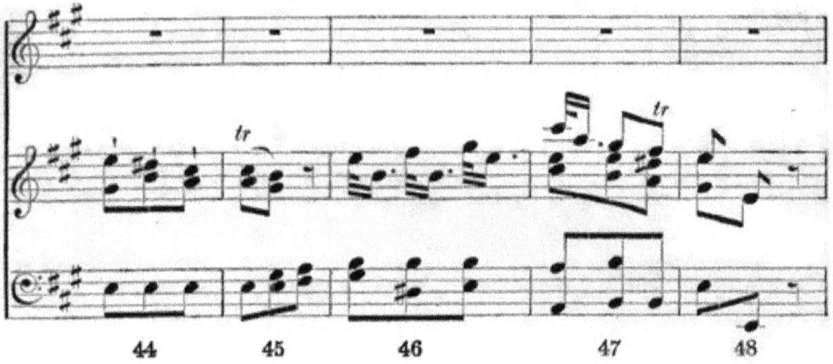
tr
tr
44 45 46 47 48

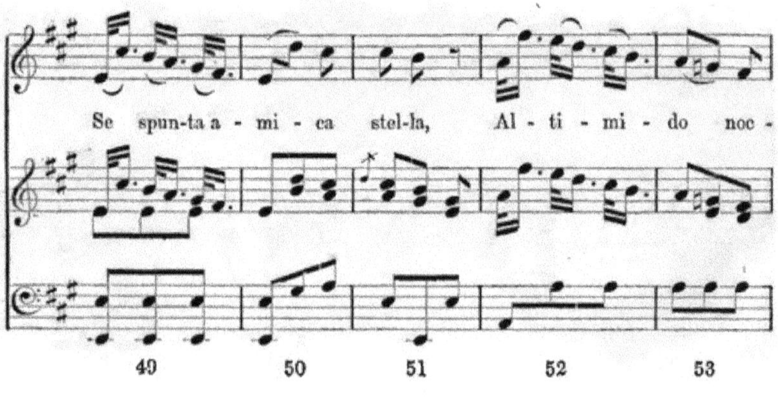
Se spun-ta a - mi - ca stel-la, Al - ti - mi - do noc -
49 50 51 52 53

- chie - ro, Sem-bra l'a - mi - ca stel - la ri - den-te e

54 55 56 57 58

bel - la, ri - den - te e bel - la, ri - den-te e bel - la,

59 60 61 62 63

Per - chè nel . . suo sen - tie - ro   nel . . suo sen - tie - ro.

64   65   66   67   68

La   cal - ma può spe - rar,   La

69   70   71   72   73

cal - - - - - - - ma . . può spe - rar, . . .

74   75   76   77   78   79

. . . può spe - rar.

80   81   82   83   84

Co - sì   quest' al - ma   mi - a,   ch'al ser - to, al - so - glio as -

- pi - ra   quel - la   bel - la   sos - spi - ra,   Col cui fa -

97   98   99   100   101

- vor de - si - a,   Sua   bra - ma a con - ten -

102   103   104   105   106

- tar,   Sua   bra - ma a   con - ten - tar.

107   108   109   110   111

Dal Segno al Fine.

112   113   114   115   116   117   118

Dal Segno al Fine.

No. 11.—*Example of the Second Variety of Ancient Binary Form.*

Air "Lascia ch' io pianga," from the Opera of "Rinaldo," by HANDEL.

- spi - ri,   e   che   so - spi - ri   la   li - - - ber -

- tà !   Las - cia   ch'io pian - ga   mia   cru - da

sor - te,   e   che so - - spi - ri la li - - ber -

- tà!

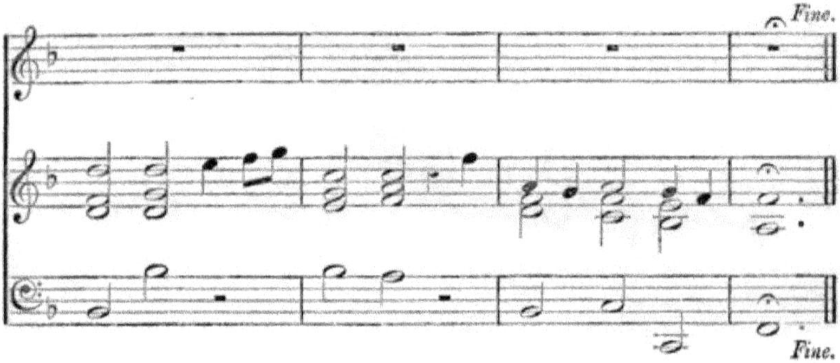
Fine.
Fine.

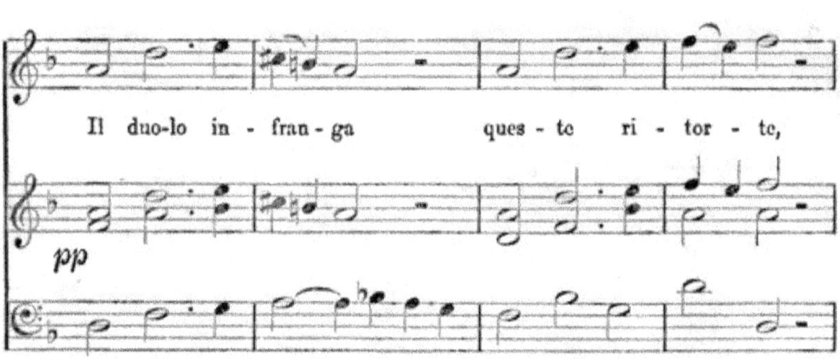
Il duo-lo in - fran - ga ques - te ri - tor - te,
pp

de' miei mar - ti - ri sol per pie - - tà, . .

Da Capo al Fine.

de' miei mar - ti - ri sol per pie - - tà.

Da Capo al Fine.

No. 12.—*Sonata in* F, *by the* REV. SIR F. A. G. OUSELEY, BART.

The following sonata has been expressly composed in imitation of the regular style of the Mozartean epoch.

The first movement is in the modern binary form.

The second movement is in the ternary form.

The third movement is a perfectly regular minuet and trio.

The fourth movement is a rondo based on the modern binary form.

The bars have been numbered, and a careful analysis has been added, by way of model.

The first subject consists of sixteen bars in the **key of F**, divided into two periods of eight bars each, whereof the former ends with an imperfect or dominant cadence, while the latter concludes with a perfect cadence in the tonic.

At the last beat of bar 16 commences the 'bridge' modulating into the key of the dominant, and terminating with the dominant harmony of the new key at bar 22.

At the last beat of bar 22 the second subject is introduced in the key of C, and in the tenor part. It is eight bars in length, and is succeeded by accessory passages, bringing the first division of the movement to a close in the key of C at bar 38.

The second division begins at bar 39 in the key of D minor, modulating perpetually, and introducing the first subject in various keys and in imitative counterpoint, until bar 52.

Bar 53 : dominant C pedal, on which are built fragments of second subject, leading back to the repercussion of the first subject, slightly varied and curtailed at bar 58.

At the fourth beat of bar 65 begin accessory passages instead of bridge, ending on dominant of original key.

At the fourth beat of bar 70 begins the second subject transposed into F, and played in the treble instead of the tenor, with slight embellishments.

Bars 78-89 : accessory passages in the key of F, intended to bring the whole movement to a brilliant conclusion.

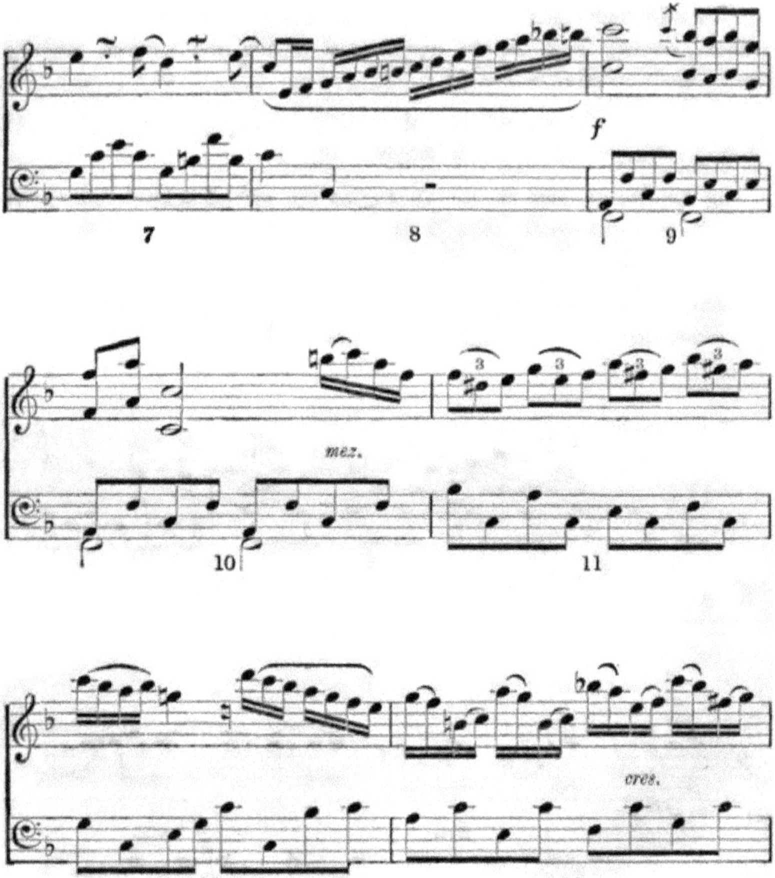
f
7
8
9
mez.
10
11
cres.
13
13

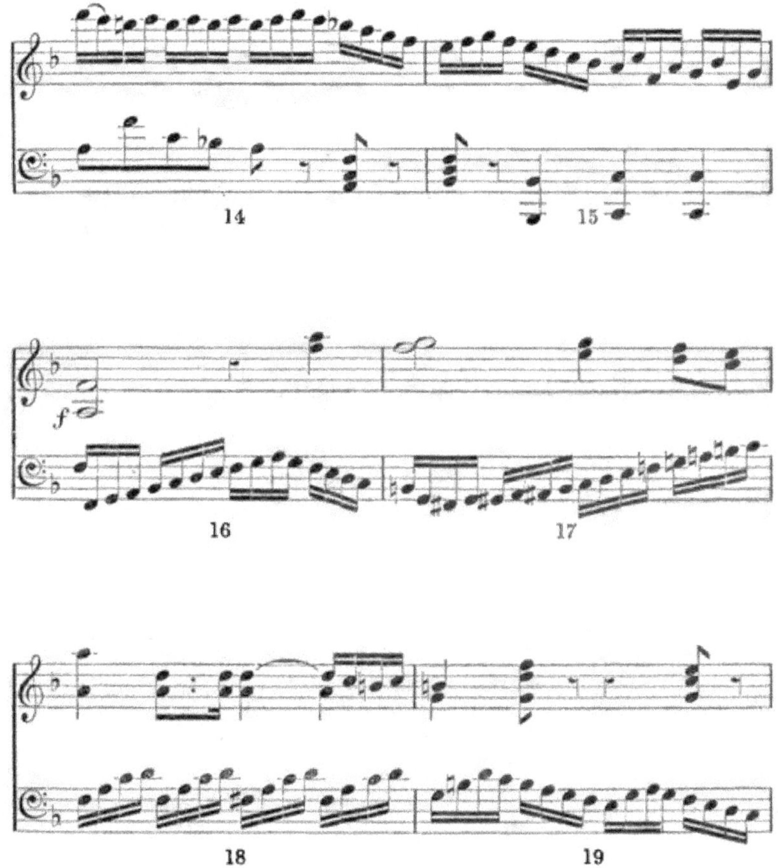
14
15
f
16
17
18
19

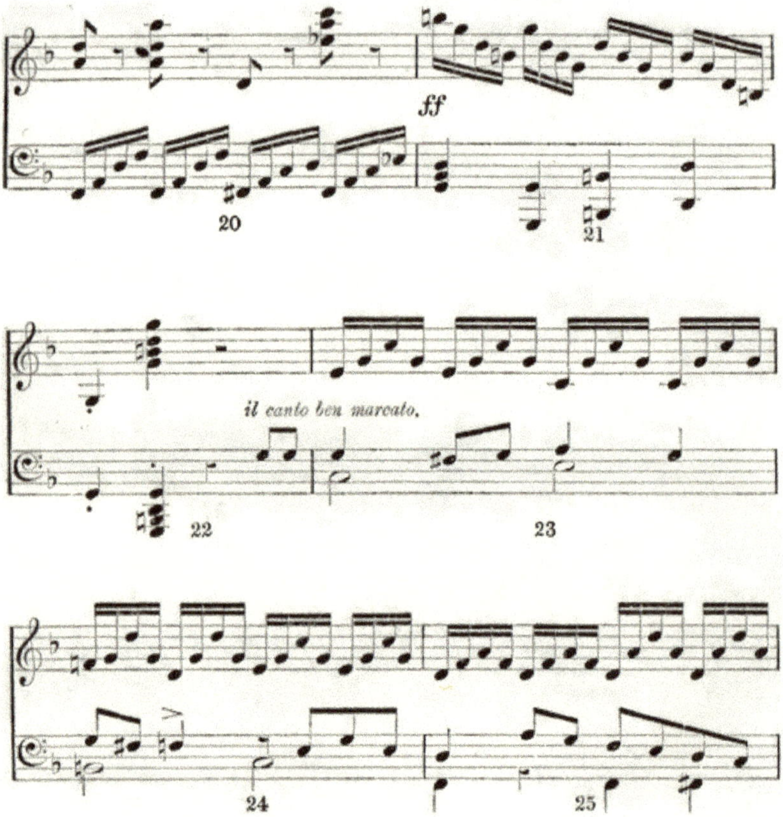
ff
20
21
il canto ben marcato.
22
23
24
25

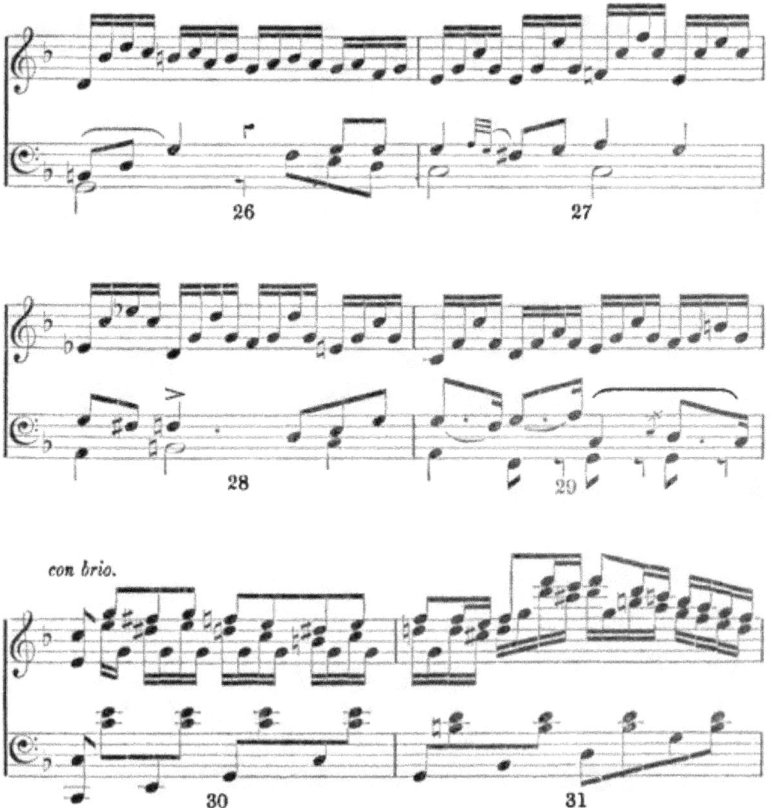
26
27
28
29
con brio.
30
31

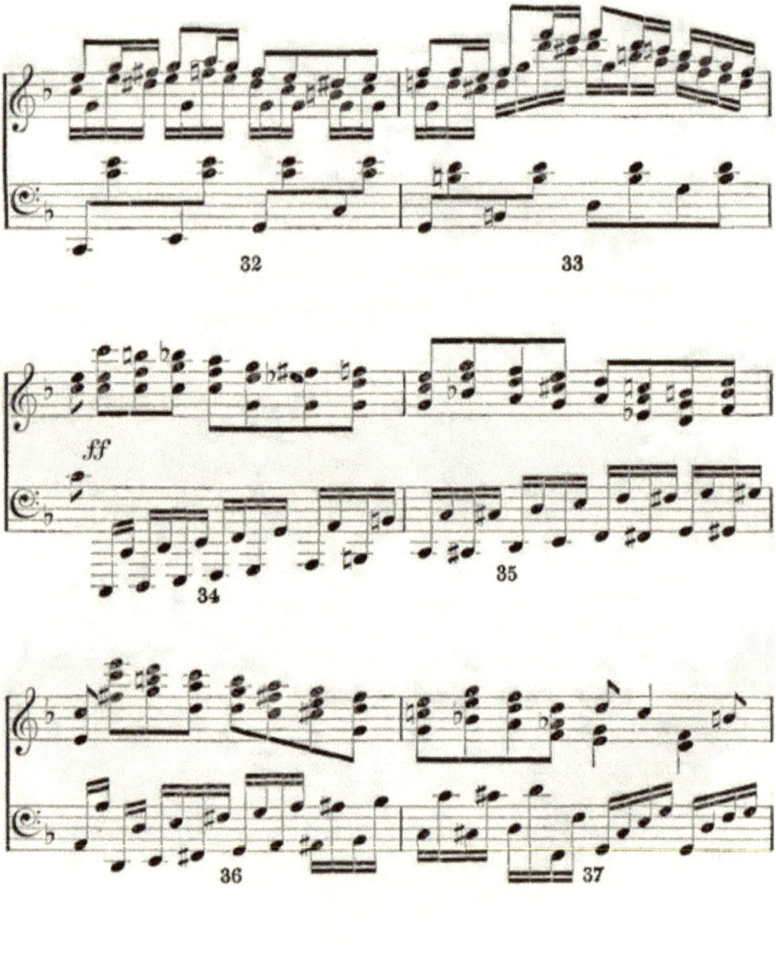
32
33
ff
34
35
36
37

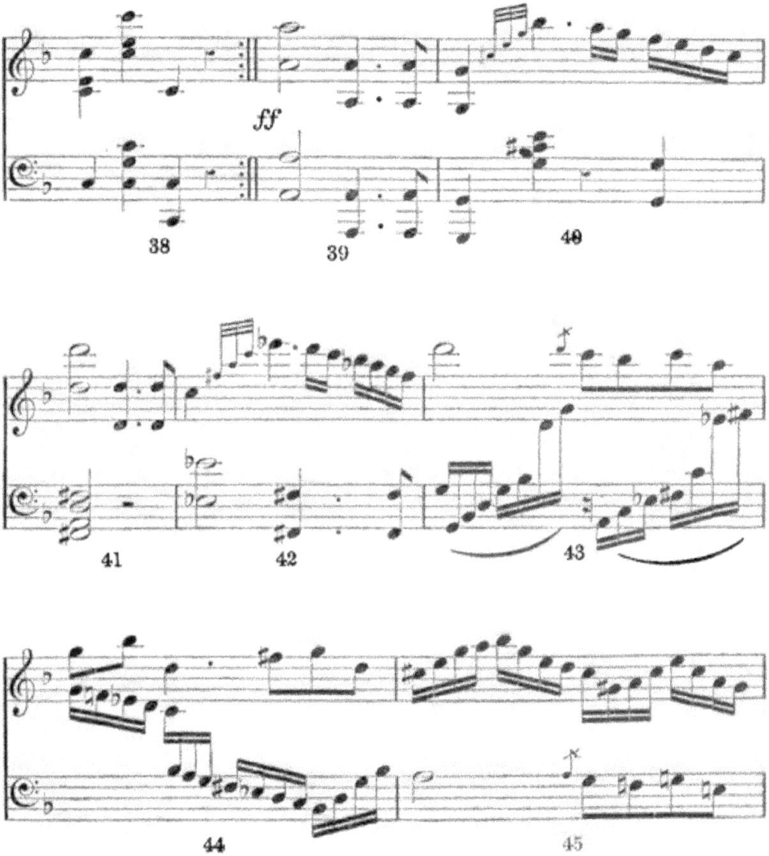
ff
38
39
40
41
42
43
44
45

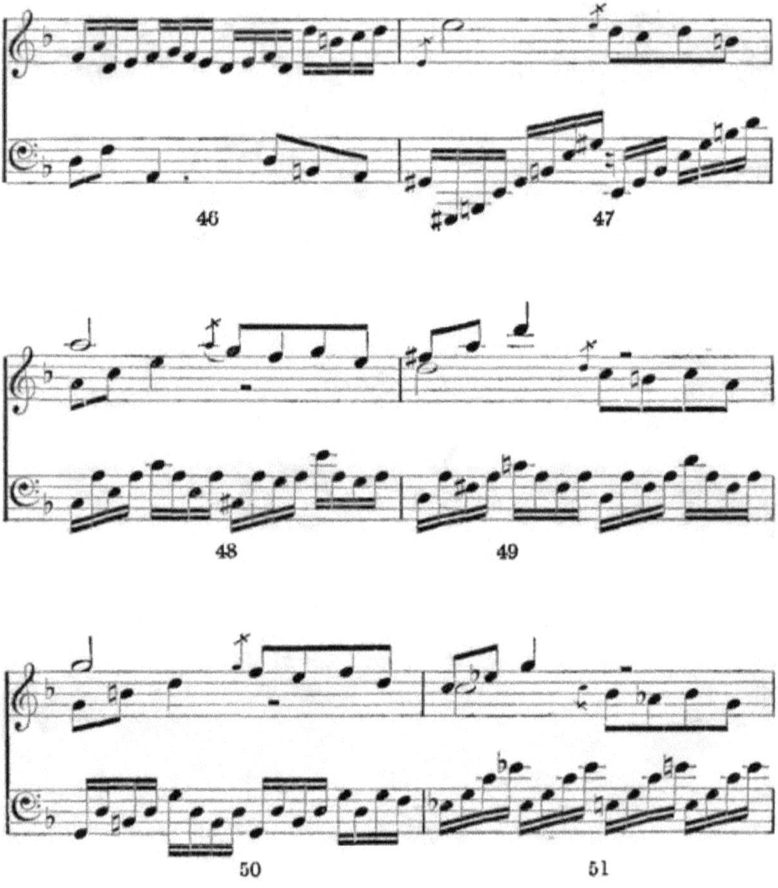
46
47
48
49
50
51

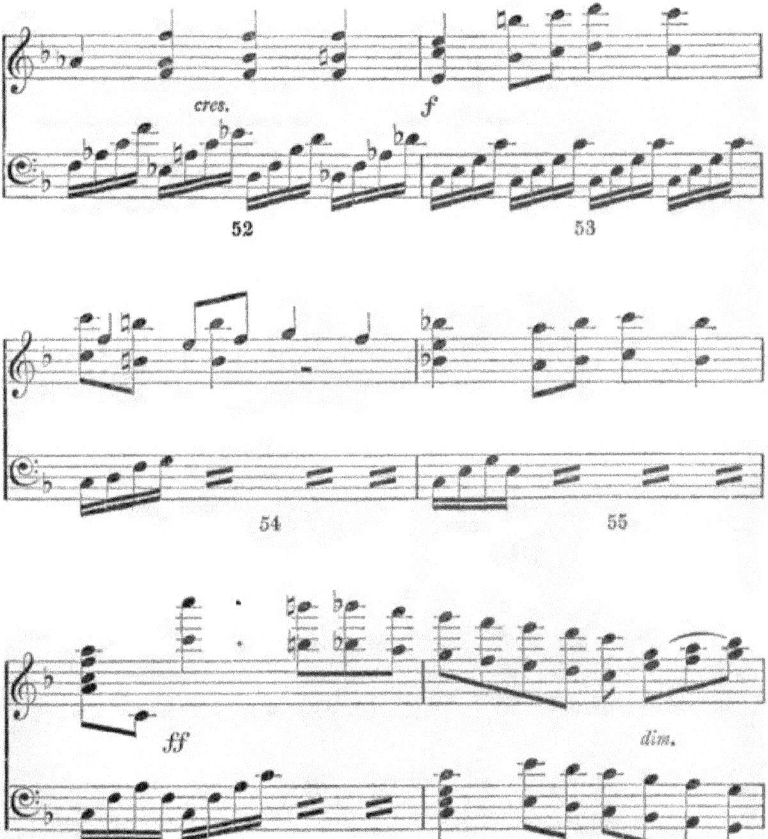
cres.
f
52
53
54
55
ff
dim.
56
57

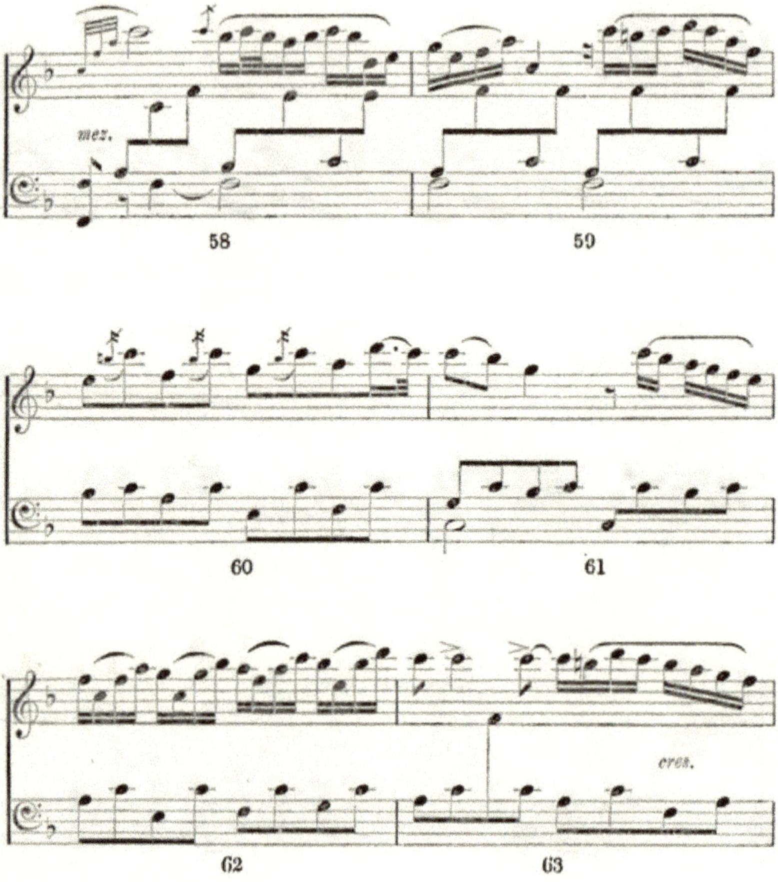
mez.
58
59
60
61
62
cres.
63

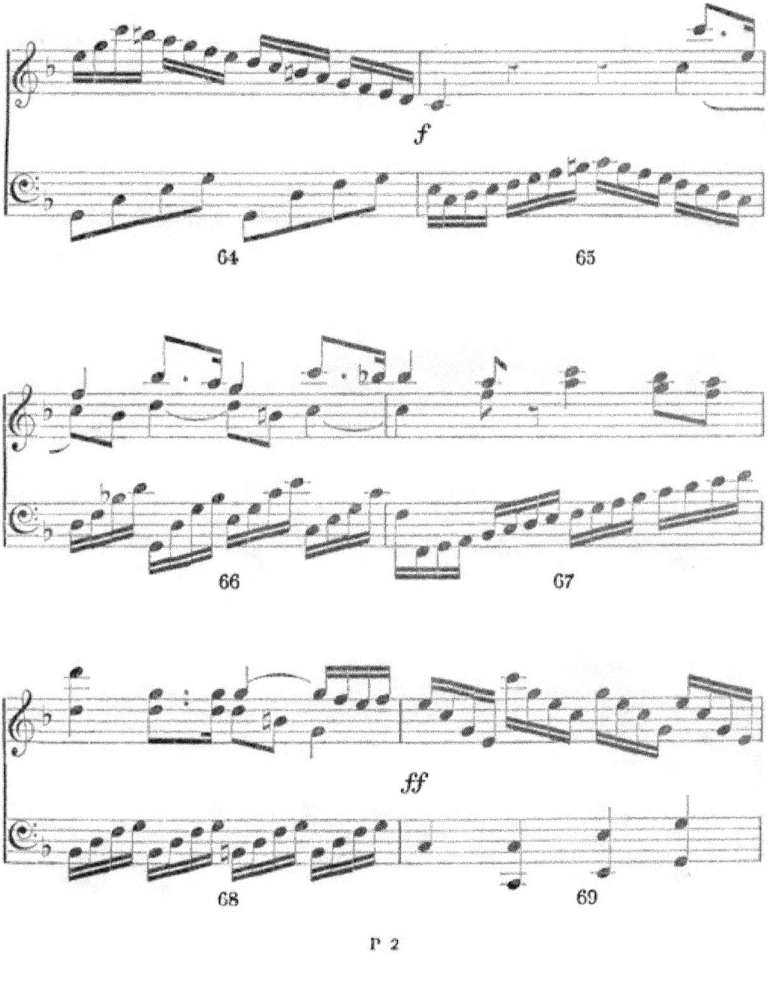
f
64
65
66
67
ff
68
69

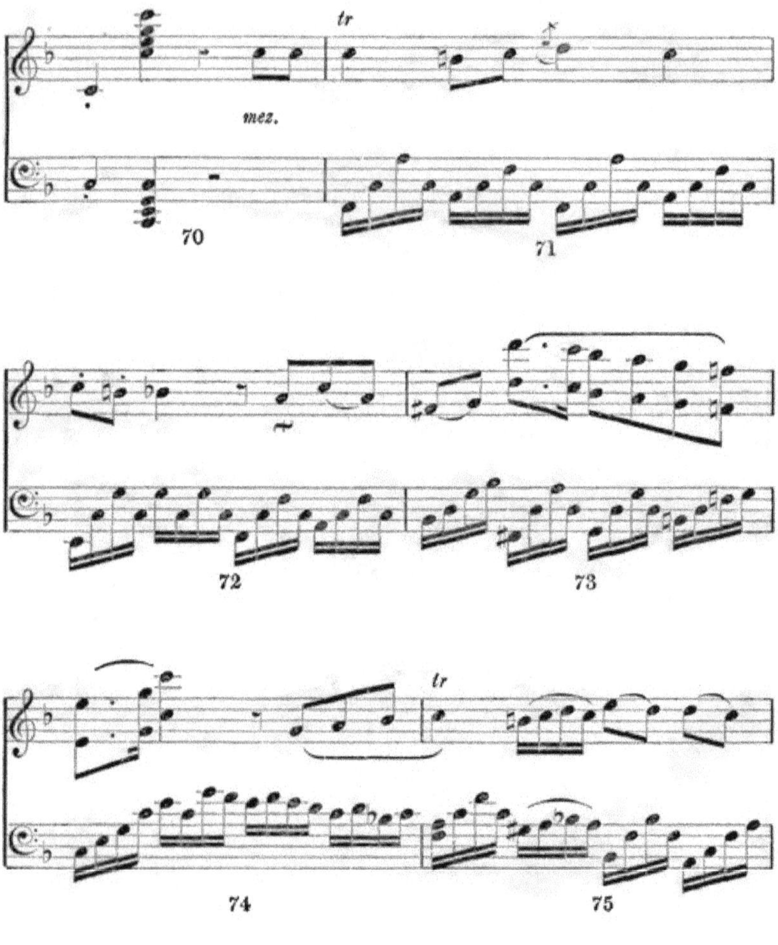
tr
mez.
70
71
72
73
tr
74
75

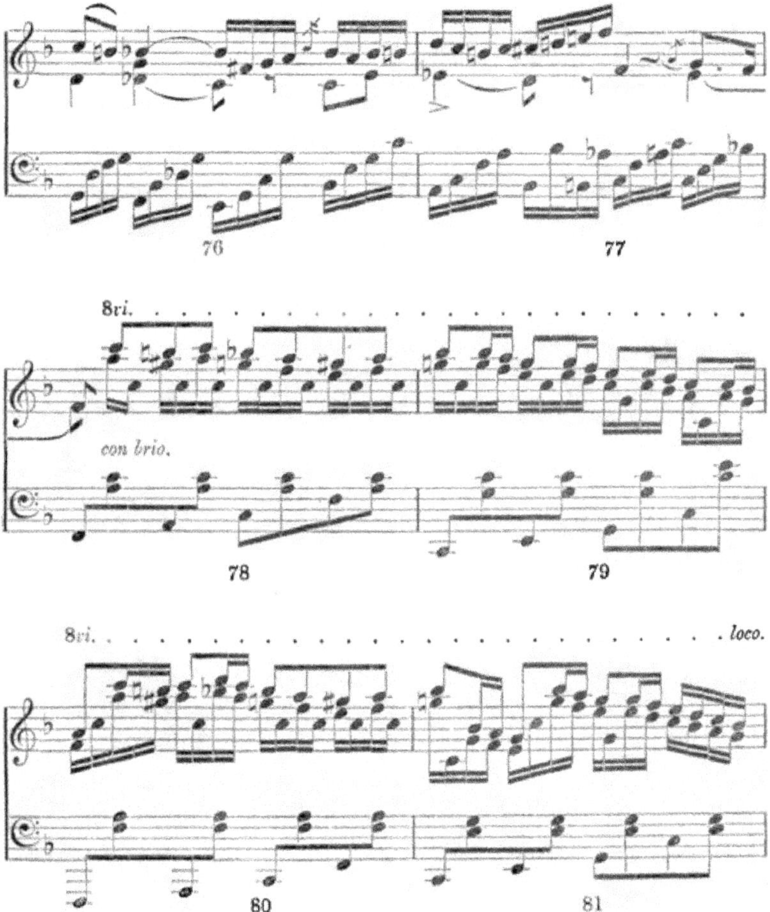
76
77
8vi.
con brio.
78
79
8vi.
loco.
80
81

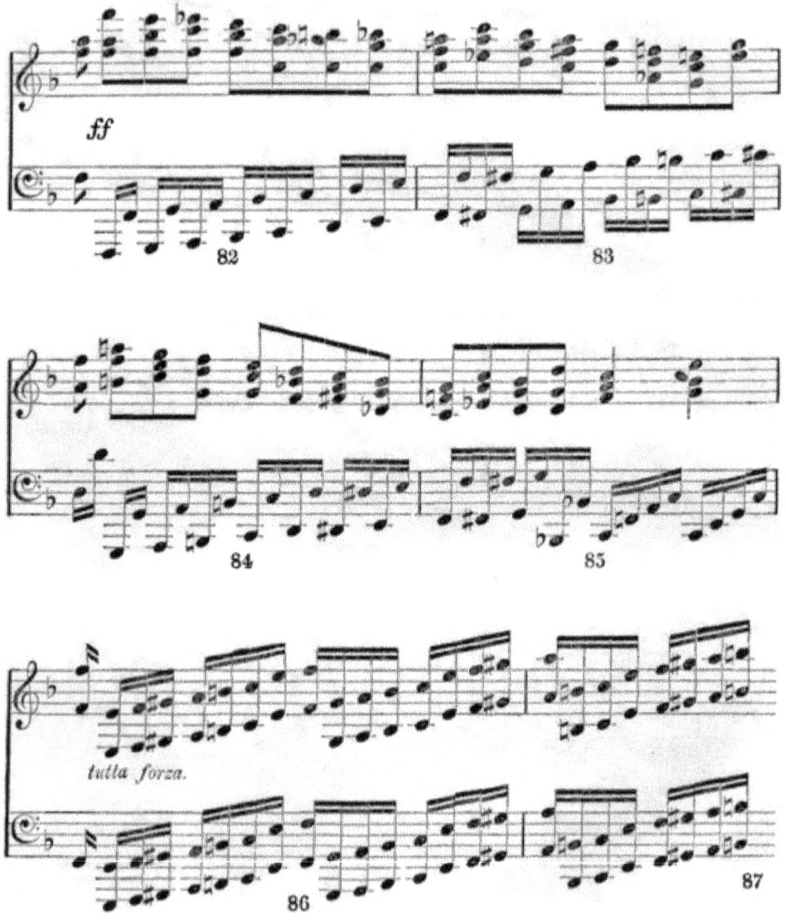
ff
82
83
84
85
tutta forza.
86
87

Second Movement.

First subject in D minor, of eight bars divided into two periods of four bars each, concluding in the key of F major at bar 8.

Bar 9: accessory subject in F, eight bars long, and modulating back again to the original key of D minor.

Bar 17: first subject repeated, but so changed as to end in the key of D minor.

Bar 24 is an interpolated bar to prolong the cadence.

Bar 26: new subject commencing the second division in the key of B flat, and keeping entirely in that key.

Bars 50-53: four bars inserted to connect the second and third divisions.

Bar 54: third division beginning and ending in D minor, and consisting entirely of developments of the preceding subjects, modulating into several keys, but returning to the original key of D minor.

Bars 79-82: three concluding bars by way of coda.

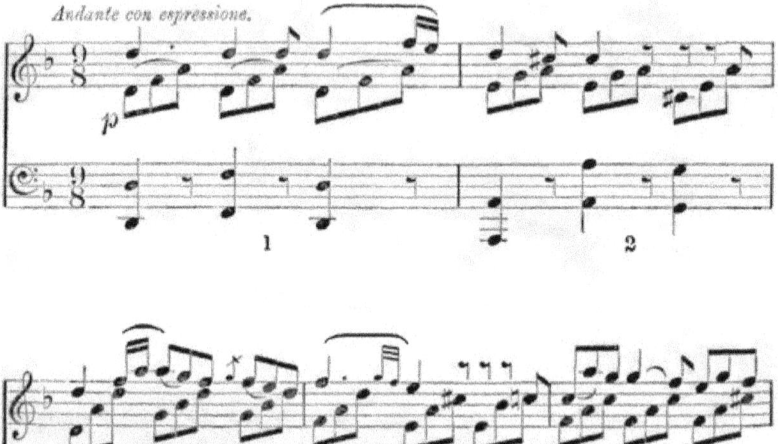
Andante con espressione.
p
1
2
3
4
5
6
7
8

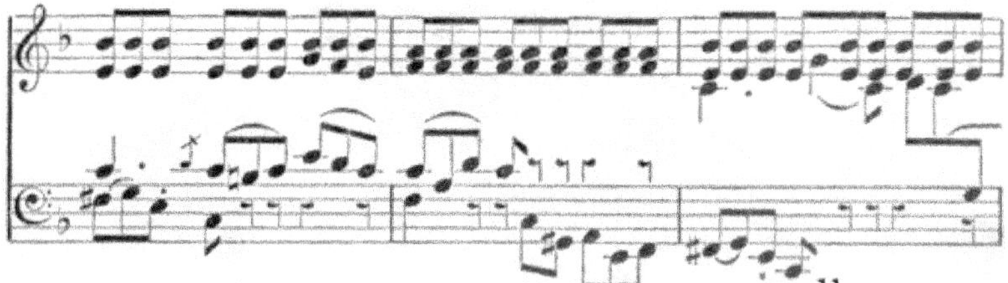
9
10
11

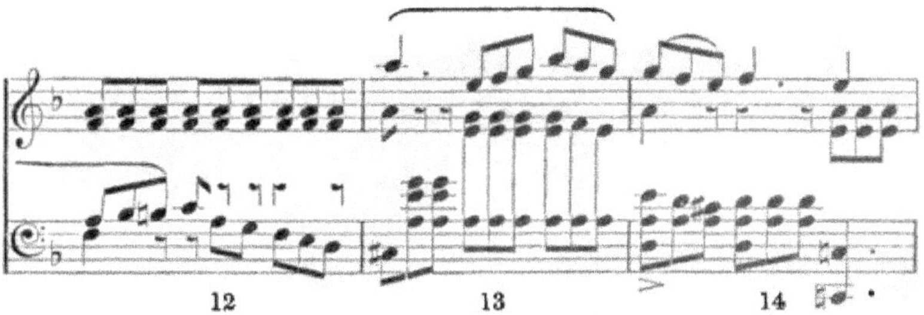
12
13
14

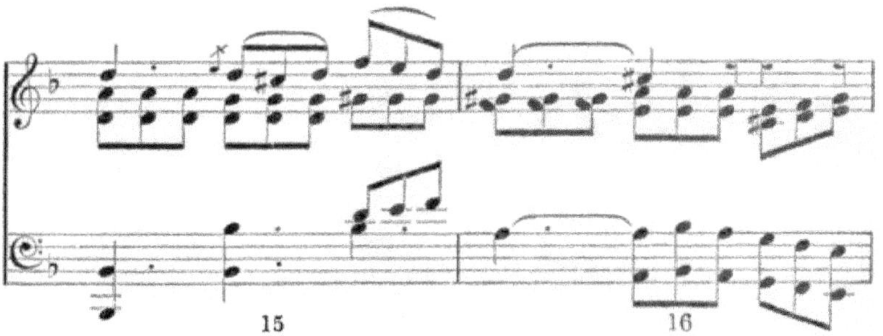
15
16

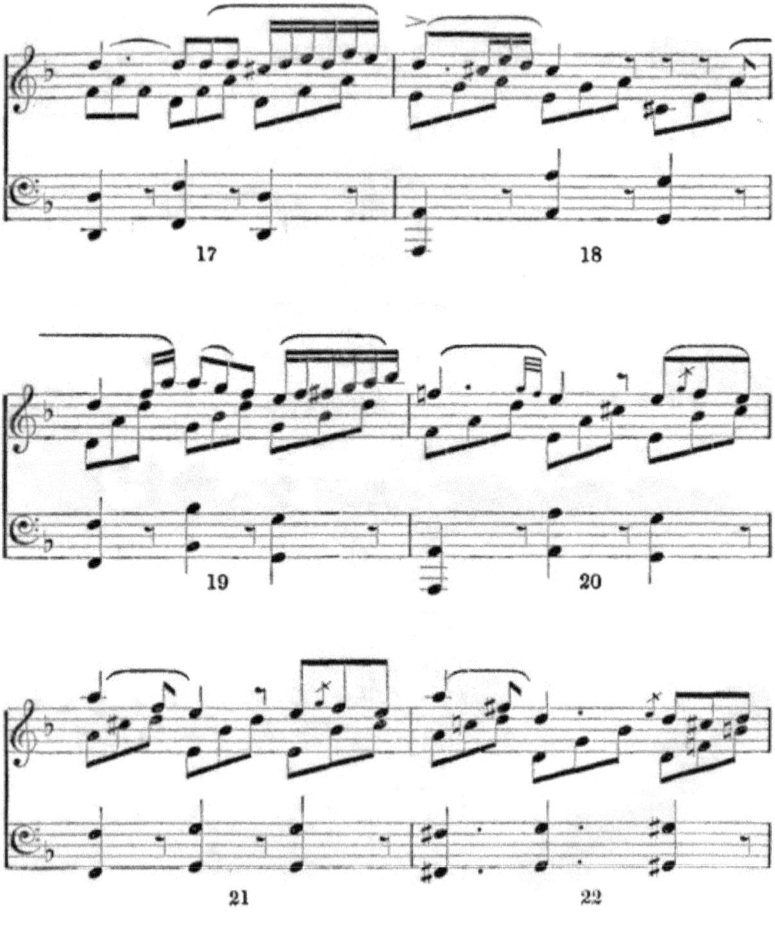
17
18
19
20
21
22

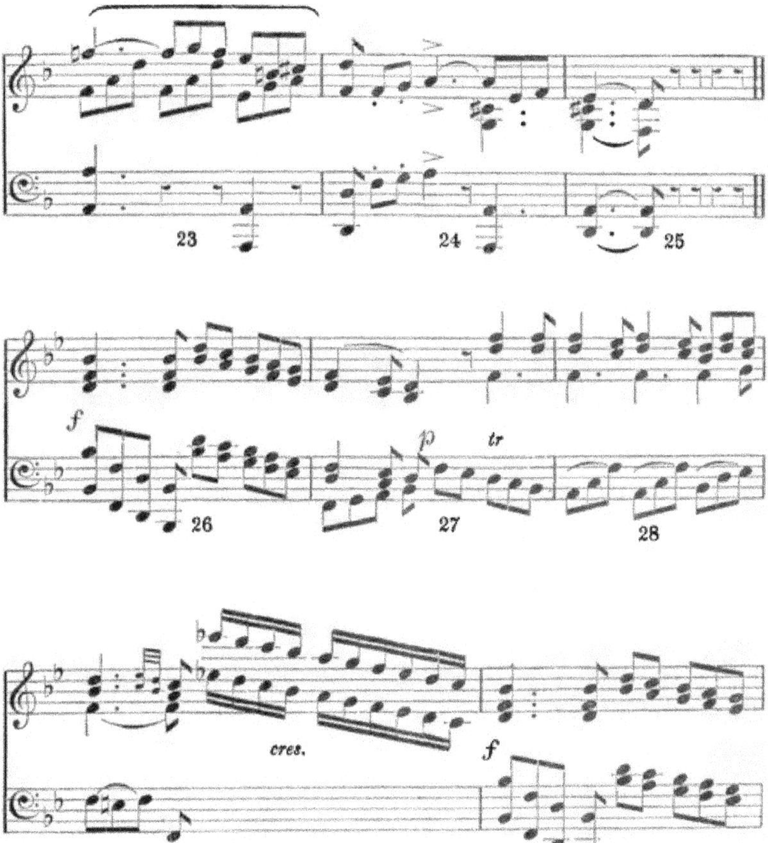
23
24
25
f
p
tr
26
27
28
cres.
f
29
30

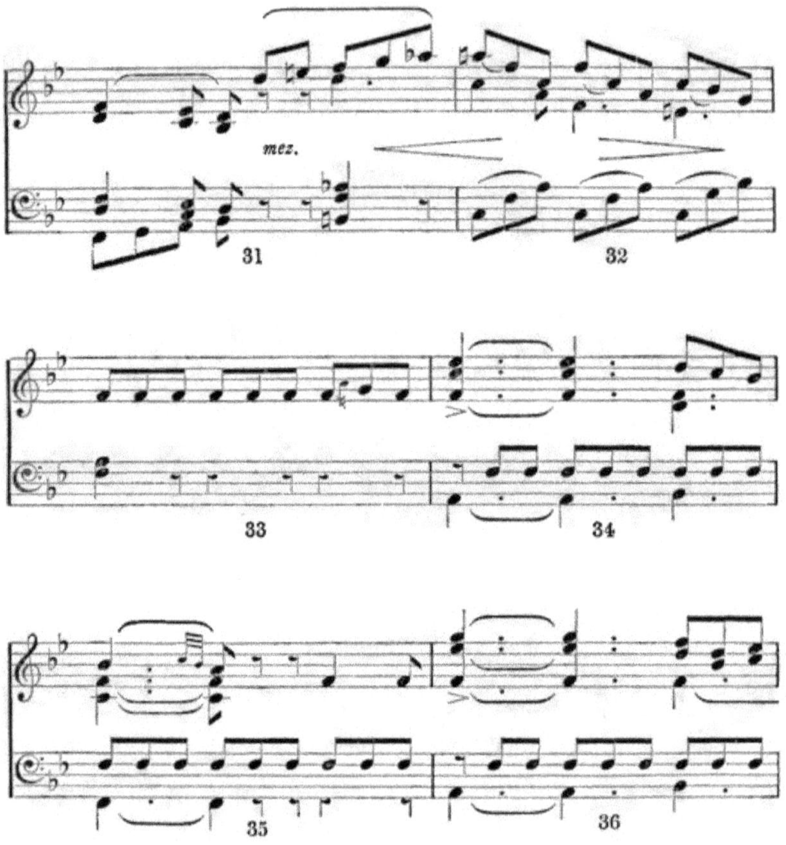
mez.
31
32
33
34
35
36

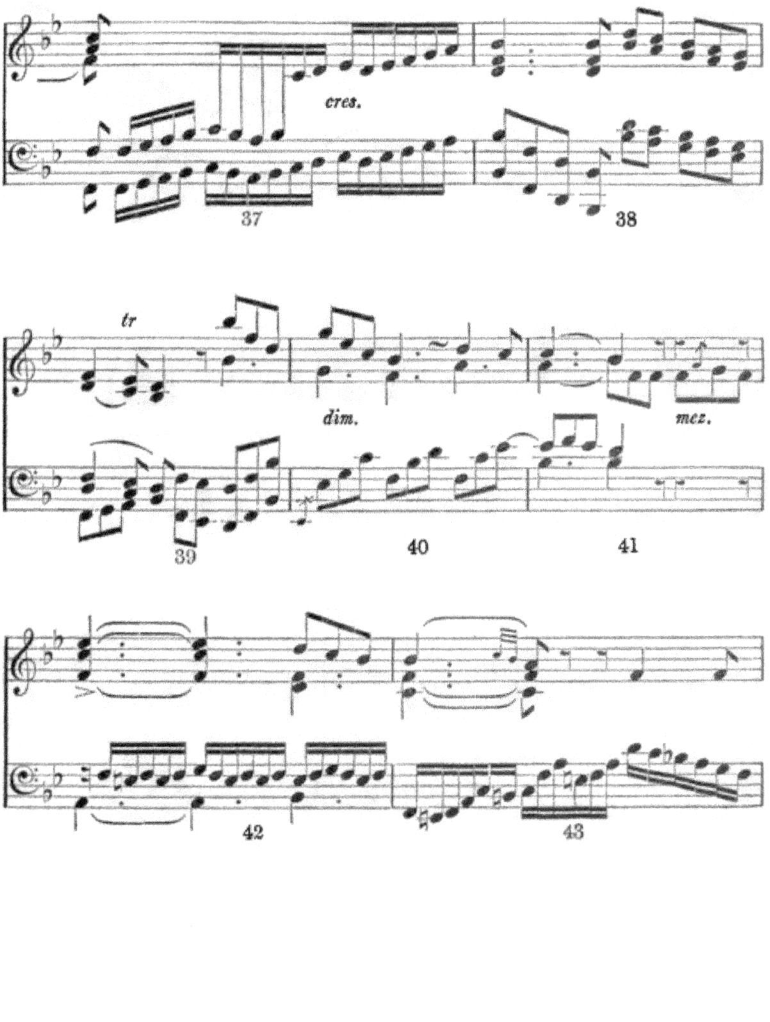
cres.
37
38
tr
dim.
mez.
39
40
41
42
43

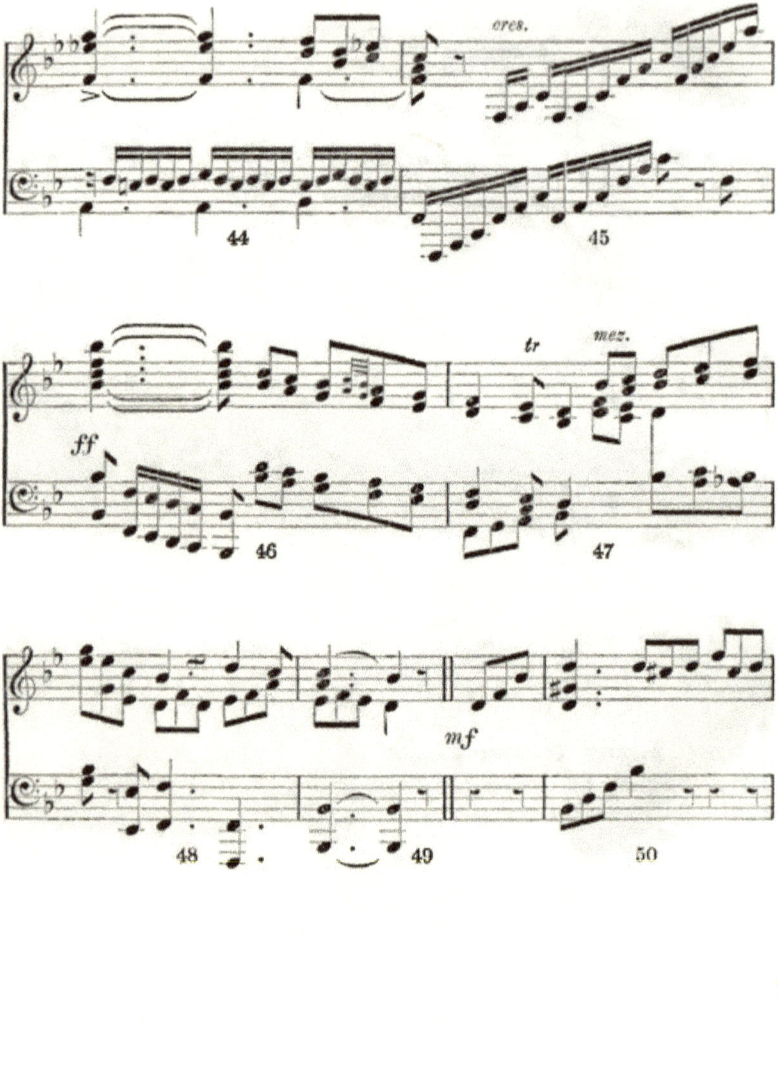
cres.
44
45
ff
tr
mez.
46
47
mf
48
49
50

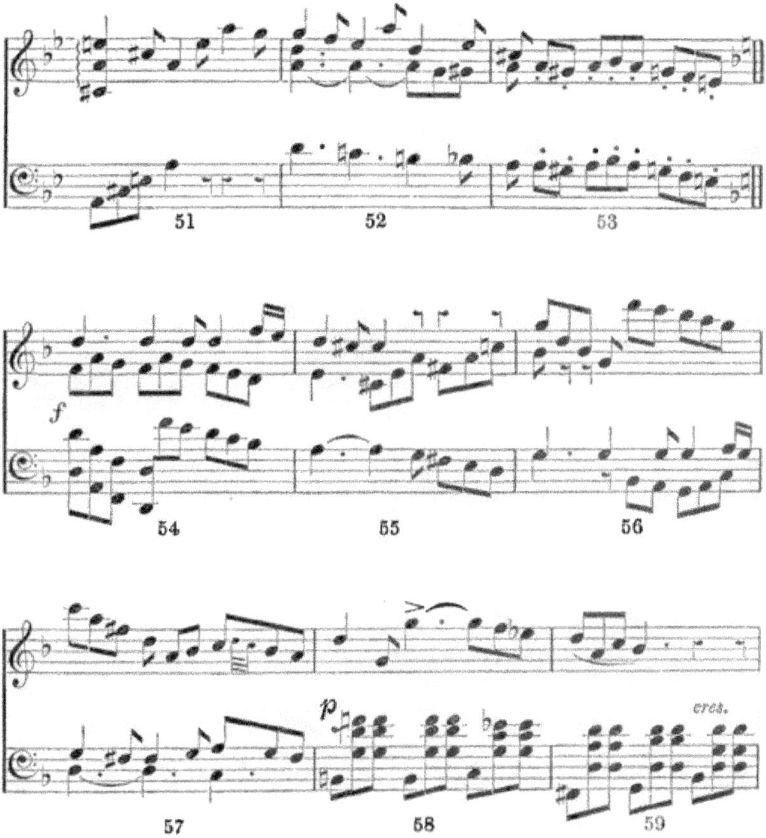
51
52
53
f
54
55
56
p
cres.
57
58
59

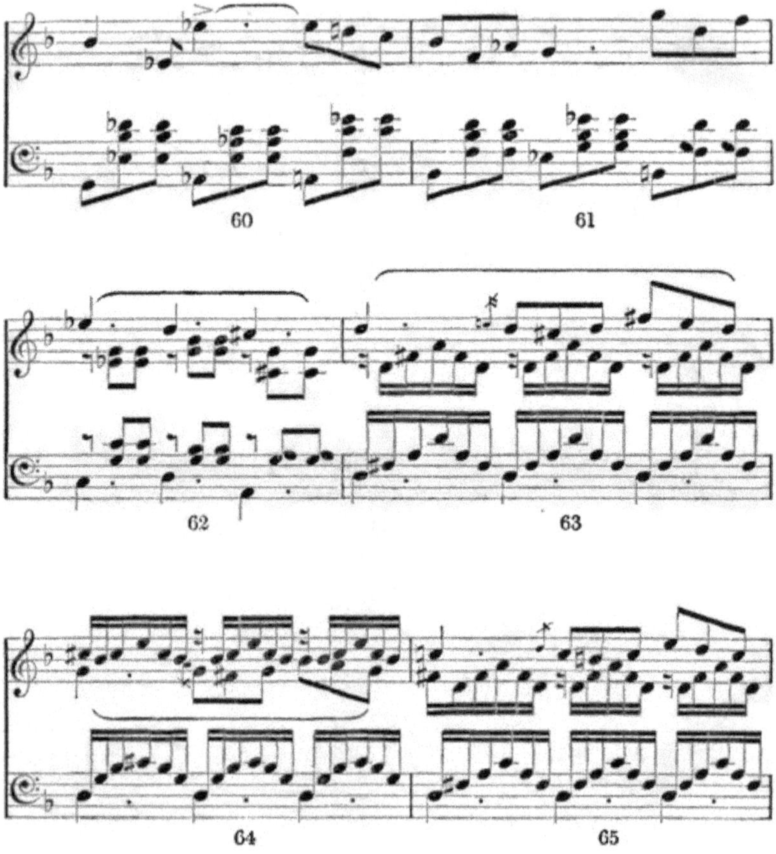
60
61
62
63
64
65

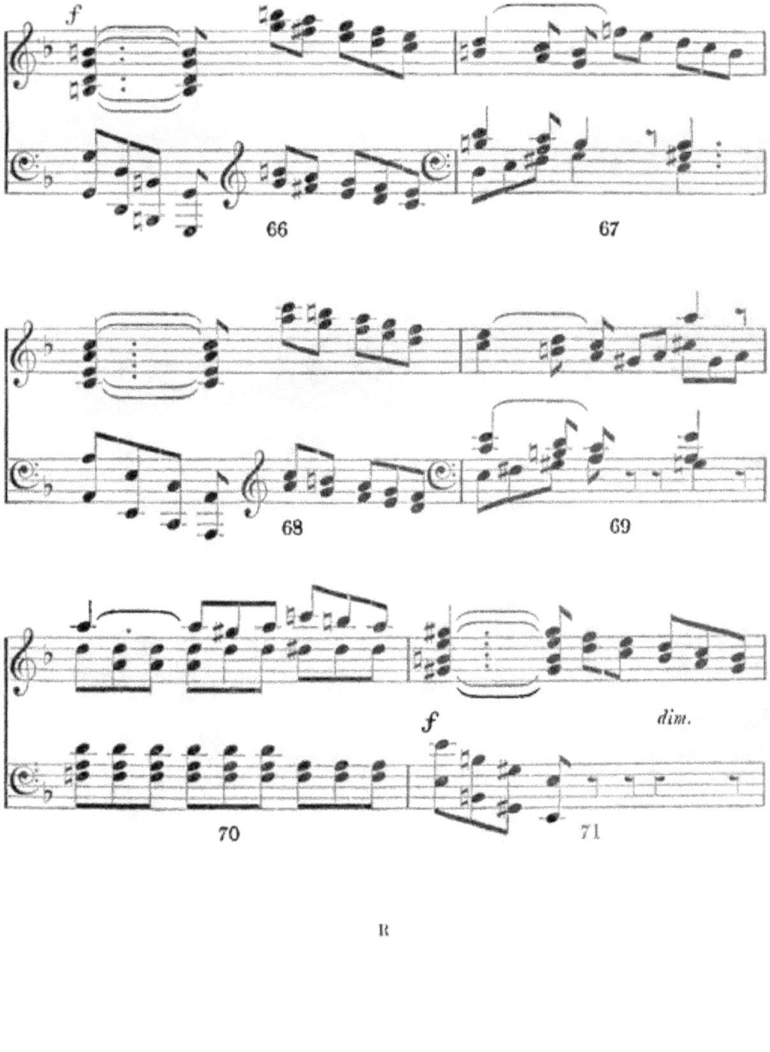
f
66
67
68
69
f
dim.
70
71

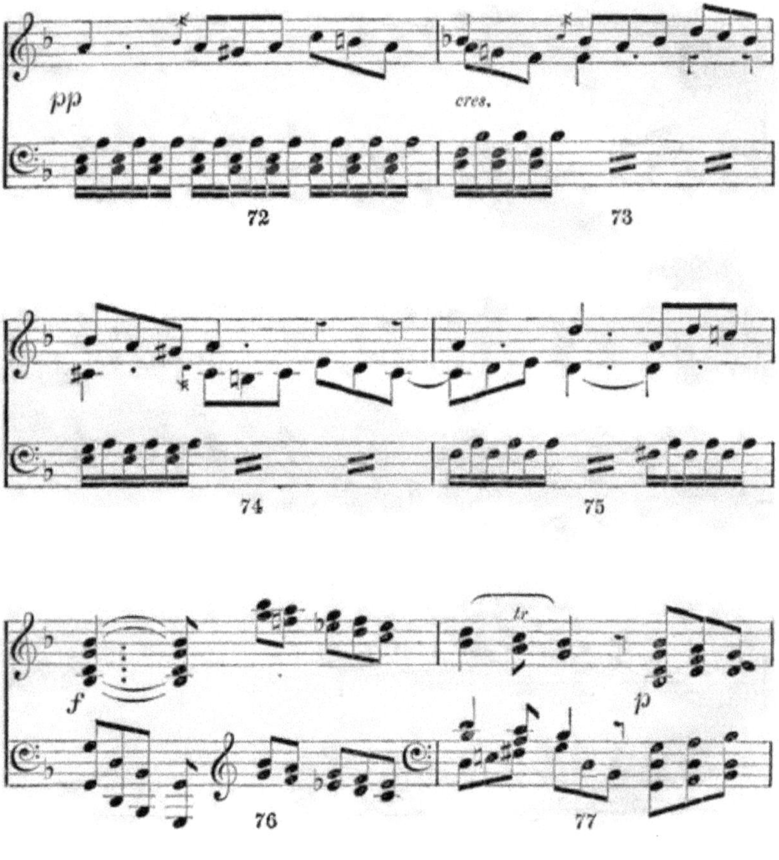
pp
cres.
72
73
74
75
f
tr
p
76
77

Minuet.

Regular minuet in the old binary form. Subject of sixteen bars, with four accessory bars in the key of F.

Bars 21–28 : Melody of eight bars, leading back to original subject.

Bars 29–40 : Original subject, but changed so as to remain in B flat ; with four accessory bars transposed into the same key.

Tempo di Menuetto, ma non troppo lento.

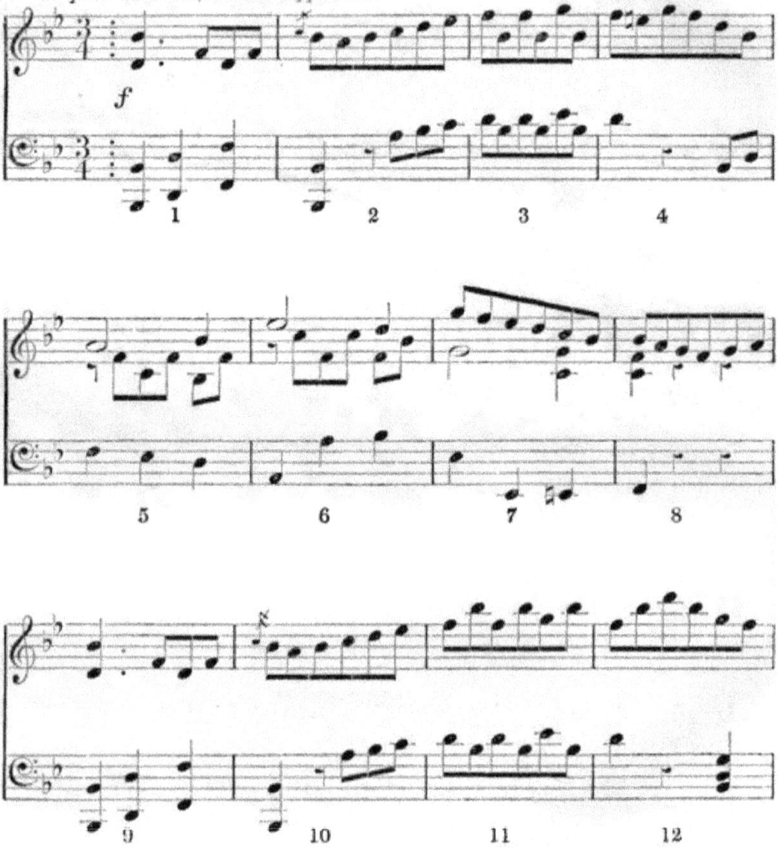

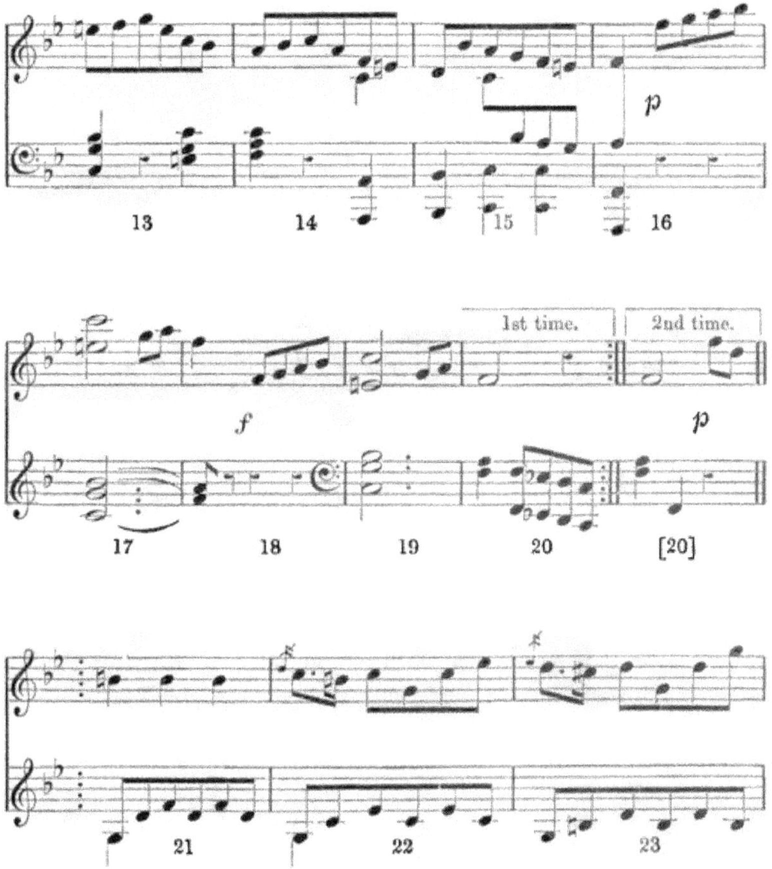
13
14
15
16
1st time.
2nd time.
17
18
19
20
[20]
21
22
23

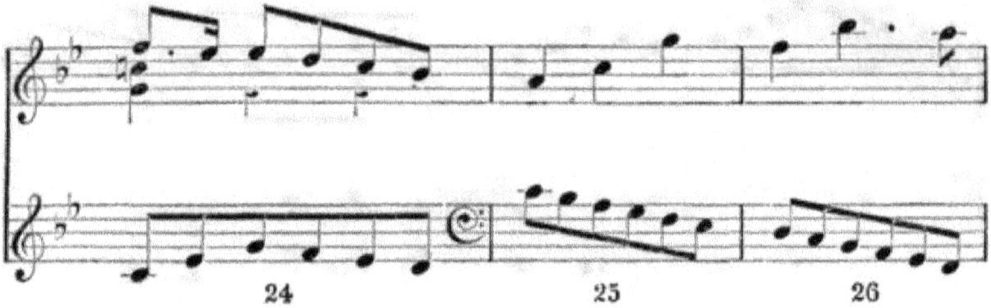
24
25
26

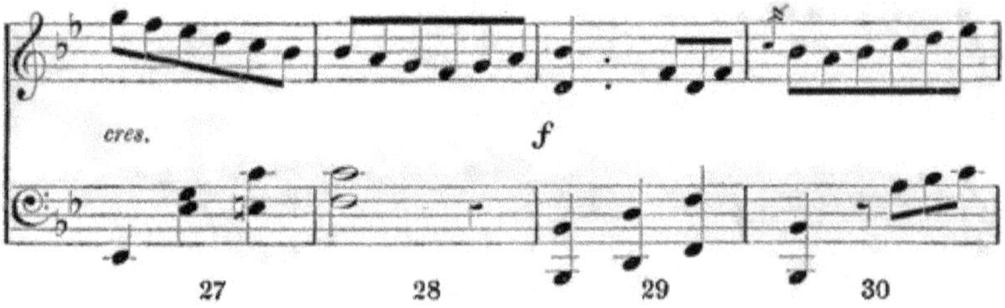
cres.
f
27
28
29
30

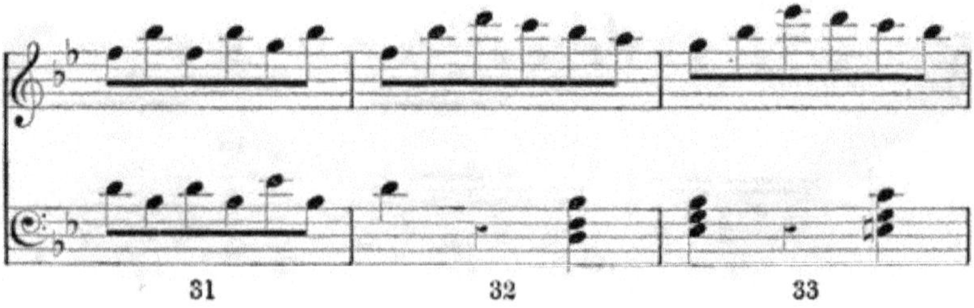
31
32
33

Trio.

Regular Trio in the old binary form. Exact counterpart of Minuet, only in the key of E flat, and with entirely new melodies.

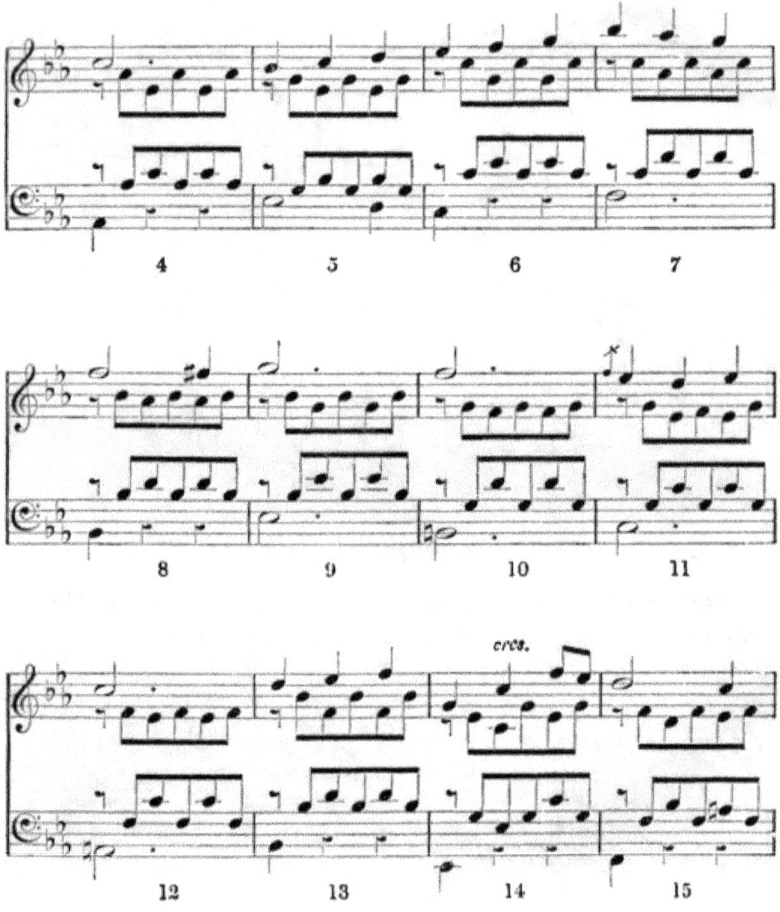
4
5
6
7
8
9
10
11
cres.
12
13
14
15

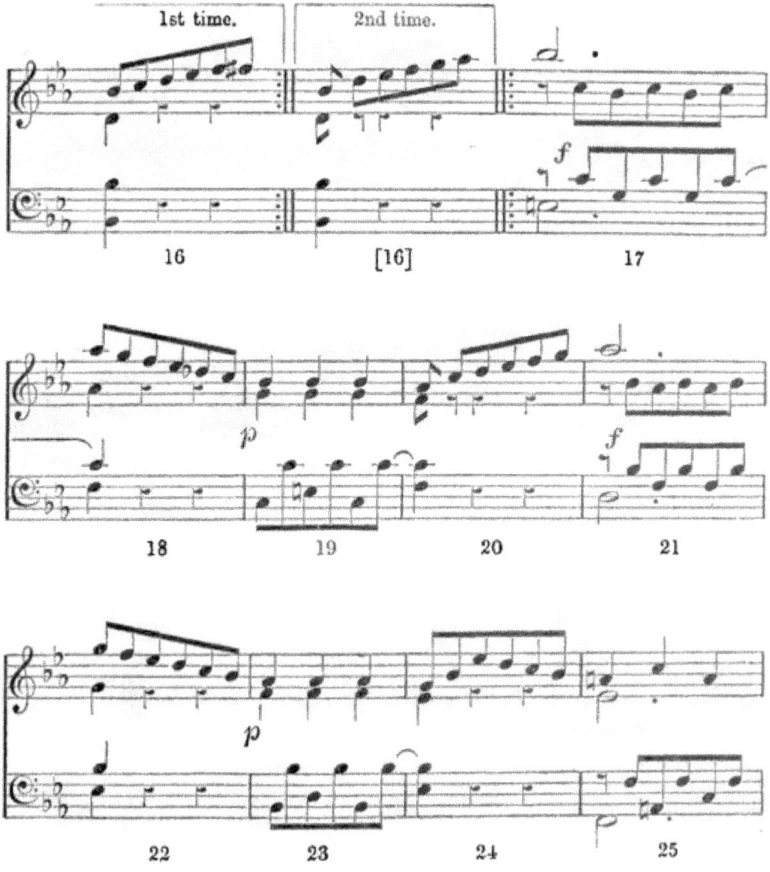
1st time.
2nd time.
f
p
16
[16]
17
18
19
20
21
22
23
24
25

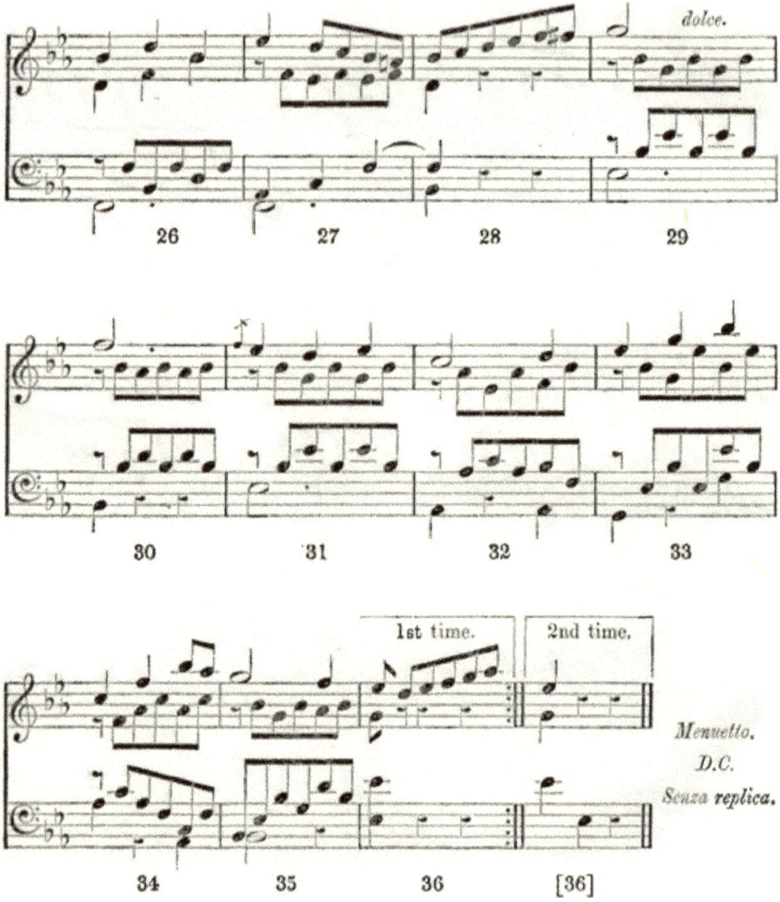
dolce.
26
27
28
29
30
31
32
33
1st time.
2nd time.
Menuetto.
D.C.
Senza replica.
34
35
36
[36]

Rondo.

Bar 1 : first subject of sixteen bars, divided into two equal periods.

Bar 17 : accessory melody of eight bars leading back to the main subject.

Bar 25 : repercussion of main subject to conclude the first sub-section.

Bar 33 : bridge to modulate into key of dominant.

Bar 48 : dominant pedal to establish the key of C.

Bar 56 : second subject of sixteen bars in the key of C.

Bar 71 : accessory passages to second subject.

Bar 80 : dominant seventh leading back to original subject in the key of F, to conclude the division.

Bar 91 : developments and perpetual modulations formed out of previous subjects and figures.

Bars 108-18 : ten bars of enharmonic modulation.

Bar 136 : dominant close leading to original subject in F, slightly embroidered, to conclude the sub-section.

Bar 154 : developments and modulations leading to second subject.

Bar 170 : dominant pedal.

Bar 181 : second subject transposed into F.

Bar 196 : accessory passages by way of conclusion.

8vi.
Allegretto vivace.
tr
tr
mez.
1
2
3
4
5
loco.
tr
6
7
8
9
10
tr
11
12
13
14

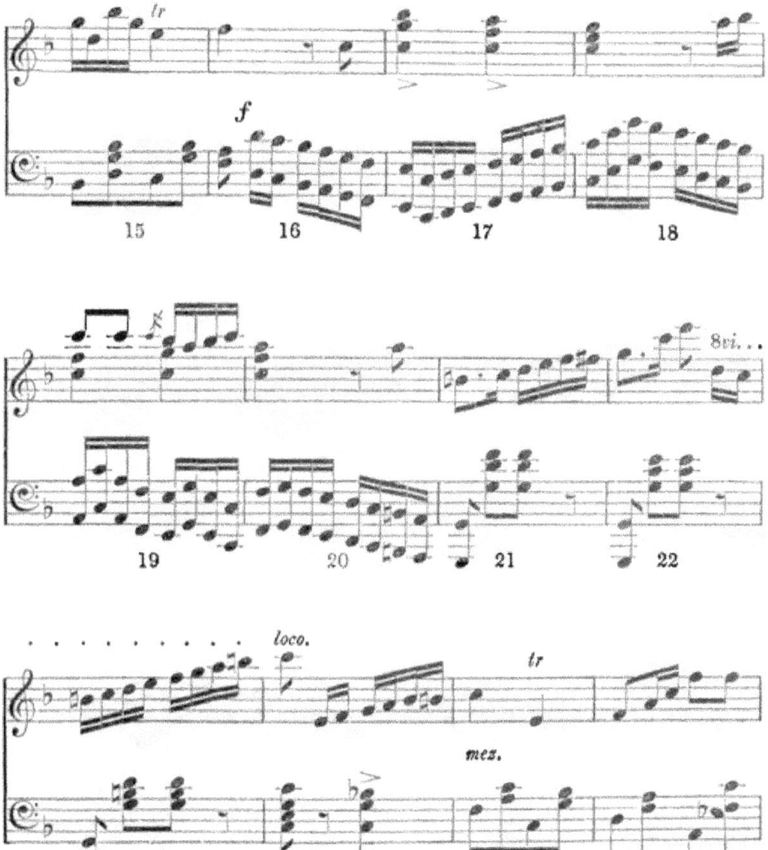
tr
f
15
16
17
18
8vi. . .
19
20
21
22
loco.
tr
mez.
23
24
25
26

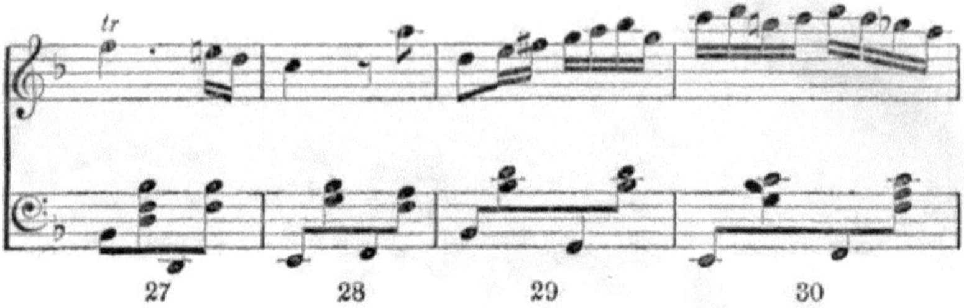
tr
27
28
29
30

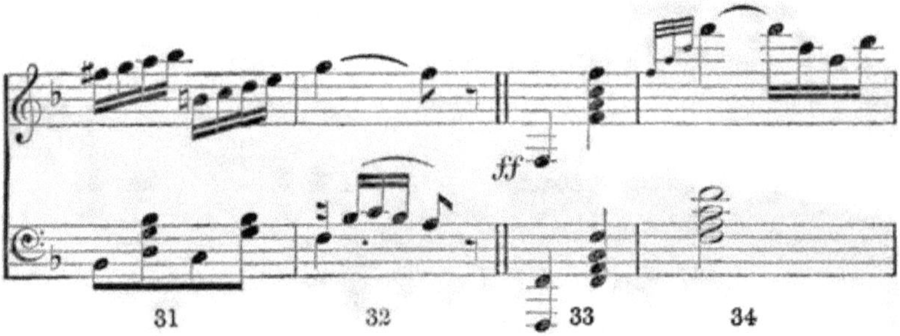
ff
31
32
33
34

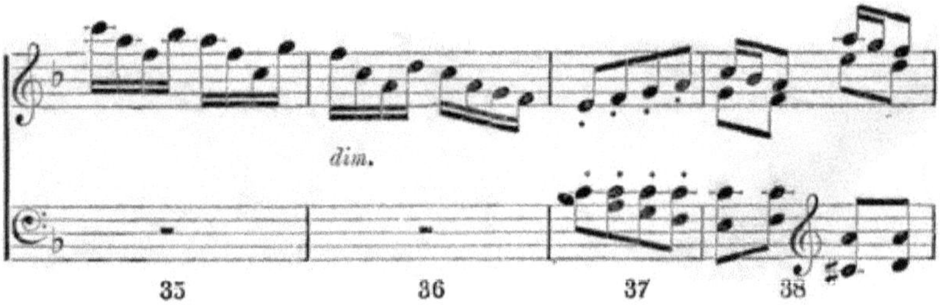
dim.
35
36
37
38

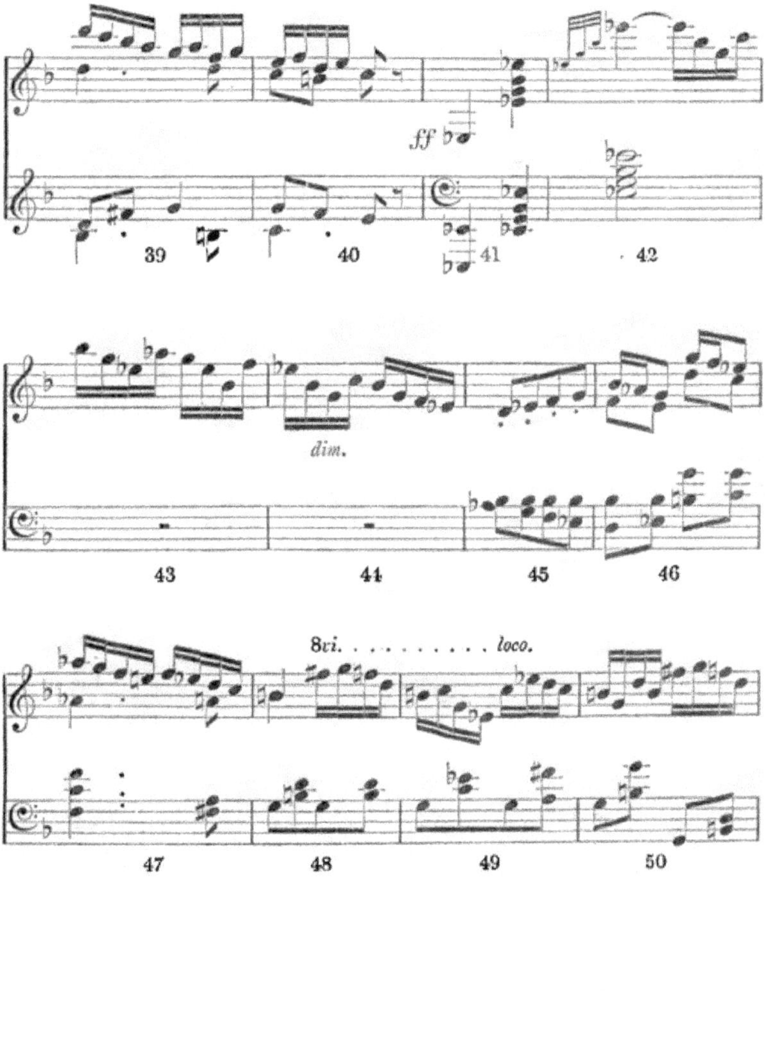
ff
39
40
41
42
dim.
43
44
45
46
8vi. . . . . loco.
47
48
49
50

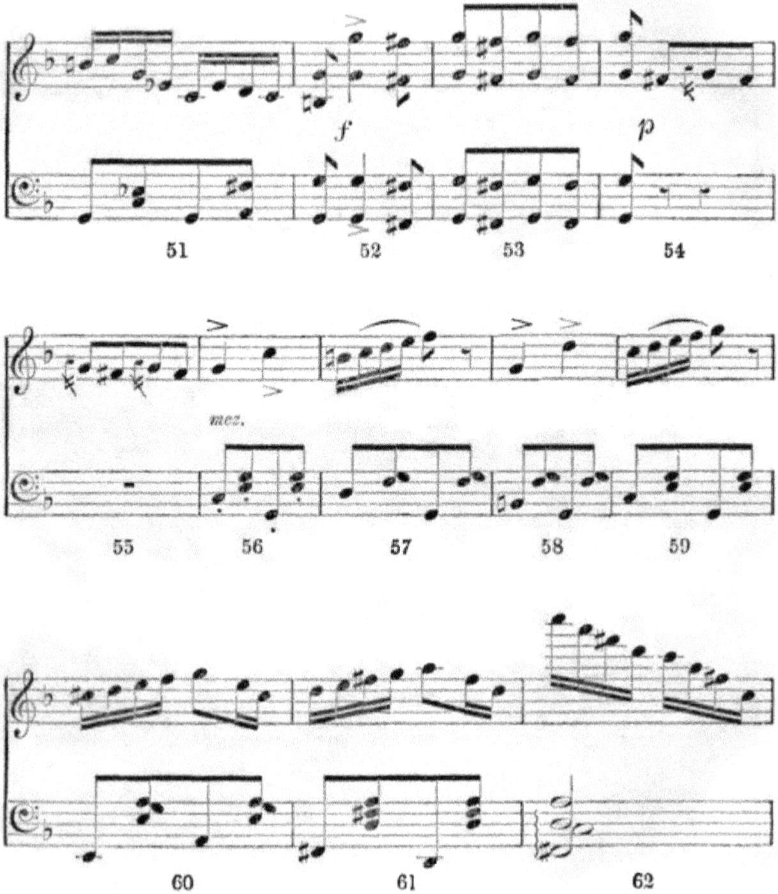
f
p
51
52
53
54
mez.
55
56
57
58
59
60
61
62

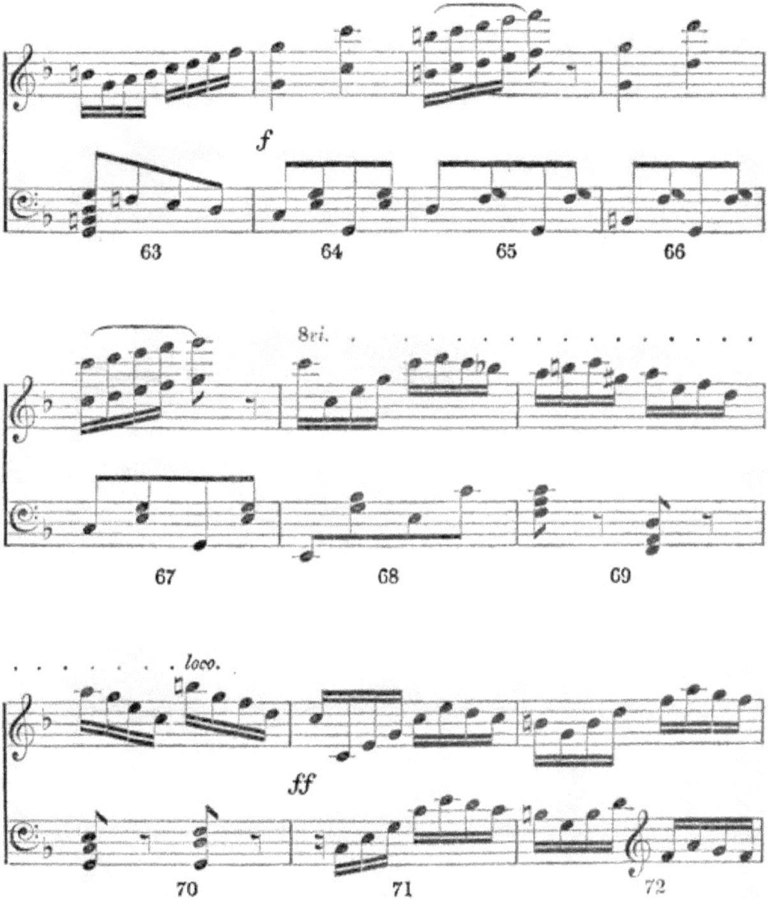
f
63
64
65
66
8vi.
67
68
69
loco.
ff
70
71
72

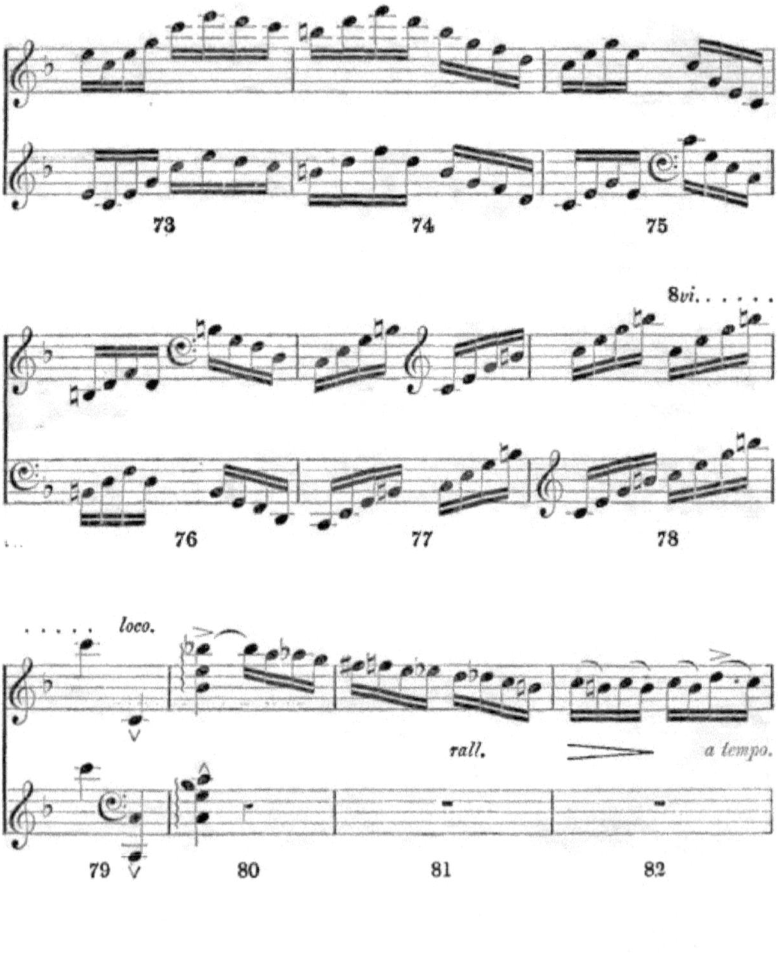
73
74
75
8vi. . . . .
76
77
78
. . . . . loco.
rall.
a tempo.
79
80
81
82

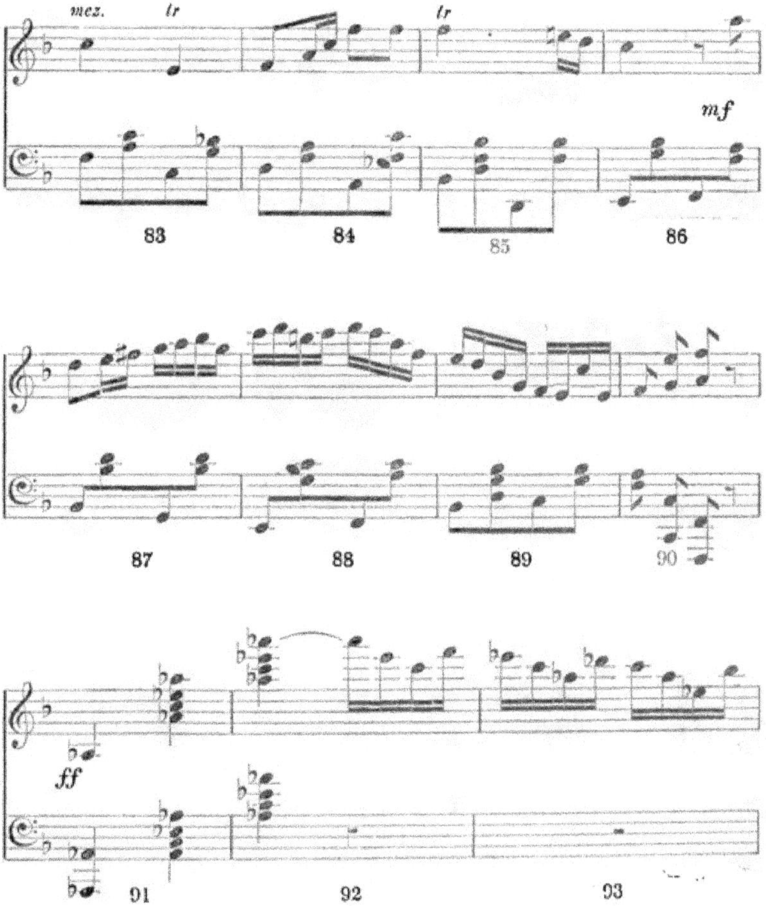
mez.
tr
tr
mf
83
84
85
86
87
88
89
90
ff
91
92
93

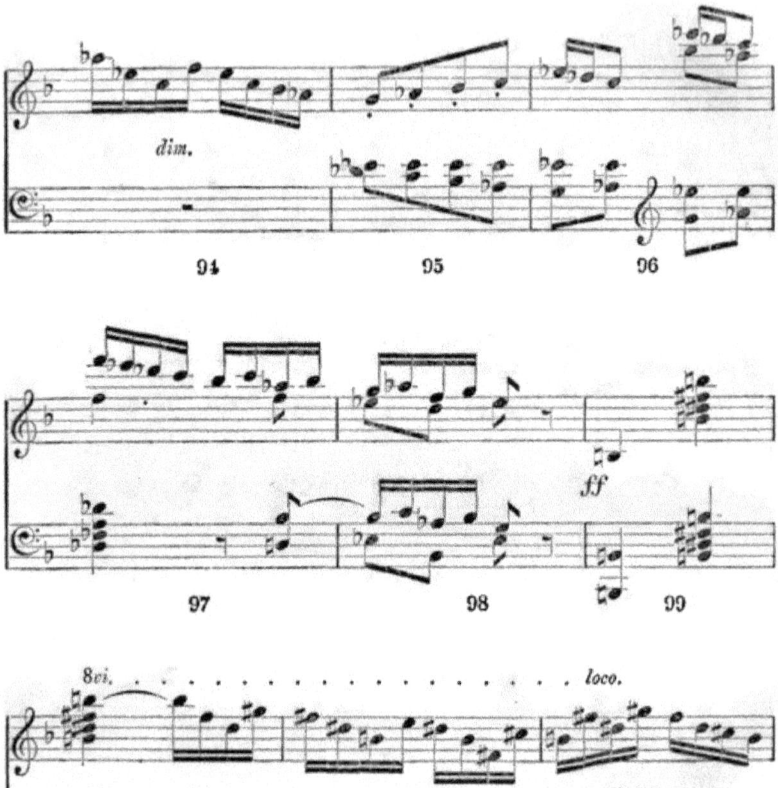
dim.
94
95
96
ff
97
98
99
8va. . . . . loco.
dim.
100
101
102

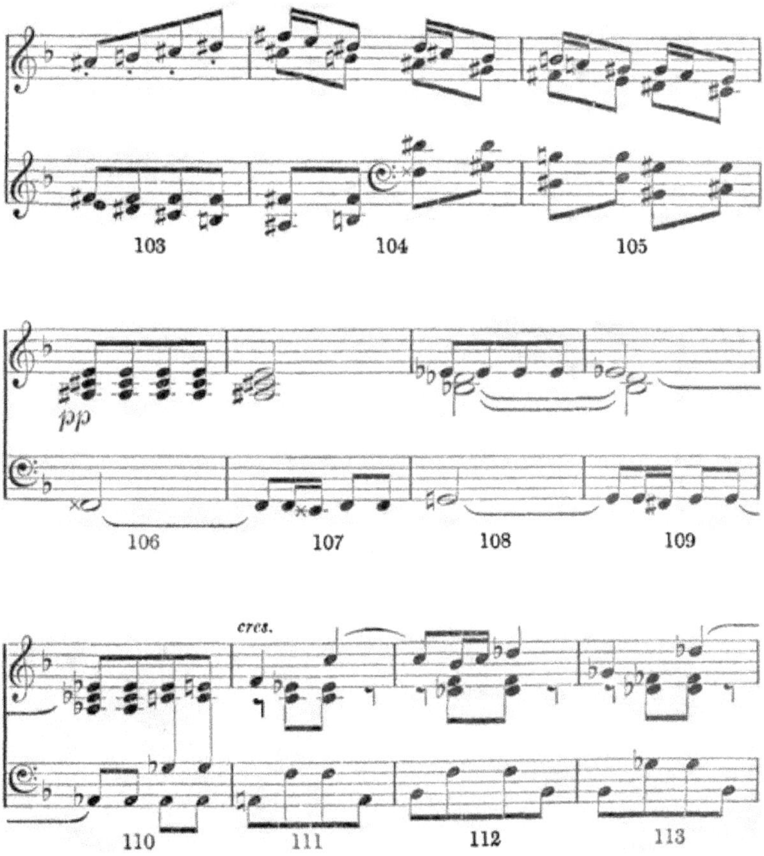
103
104
105
pp
106
107
108
109
cres.
110
111
112
113

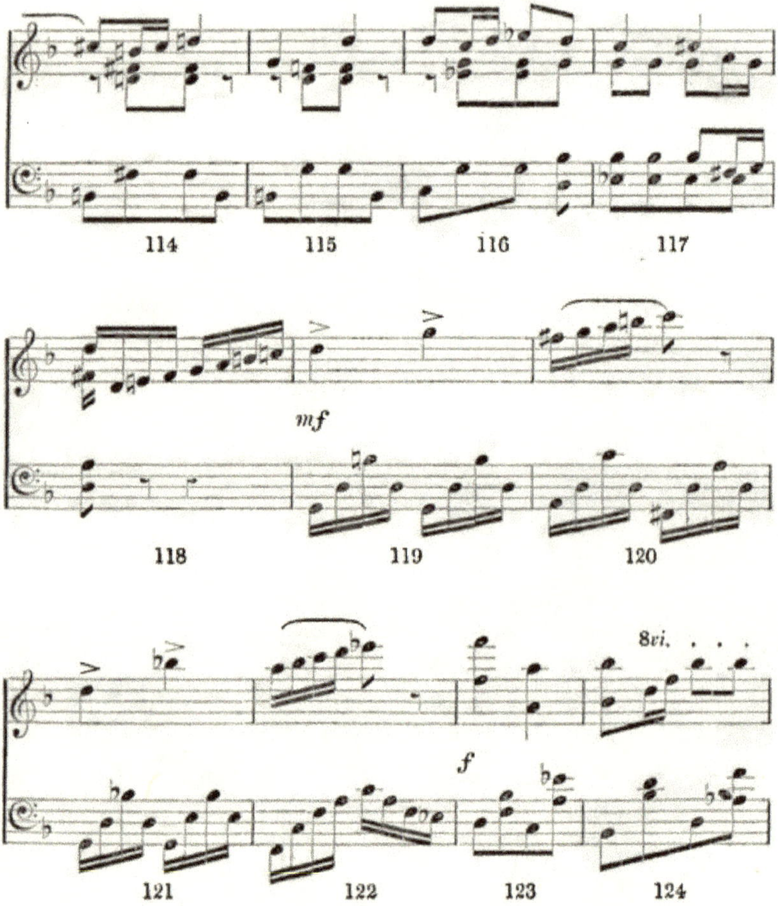
114
115
116
117
mf
118
119
120
8vi. . . .
f
121
122
123
124

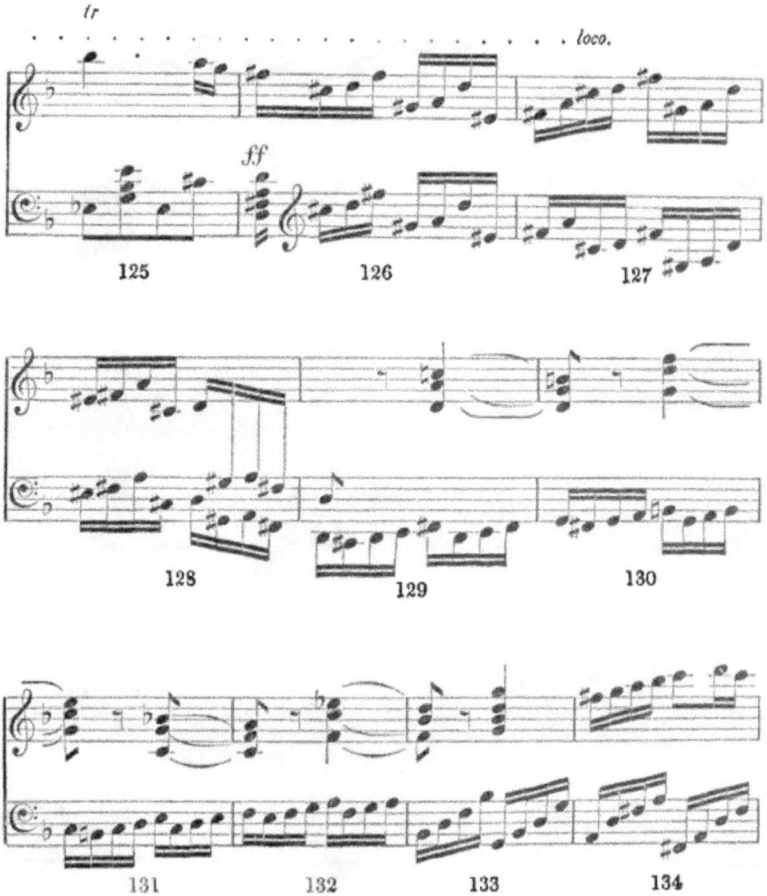
tr
loco.
ff
125
126
127
128
129
130
131
132
133
134

tr
mez.
rall.
a tempo.
135
136
137
138
8vi.
tr
139
140
141
142
loco.
tr
143
144
145
146

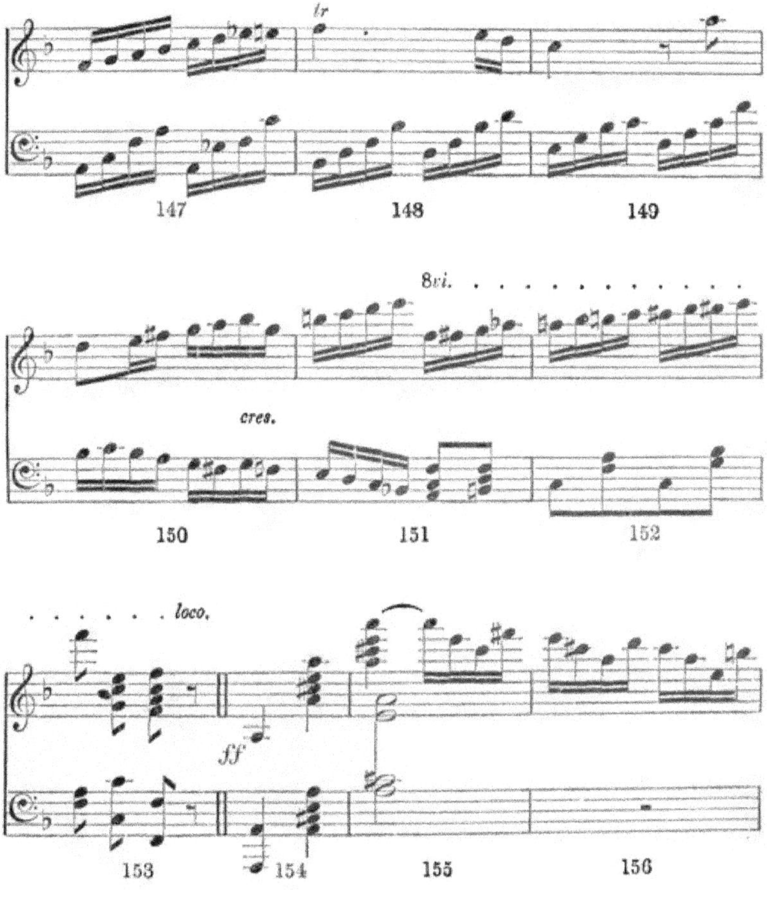
tr
147
148
149
8vi.
cres.
150
151
152
loco.
ff
153
154
155
156

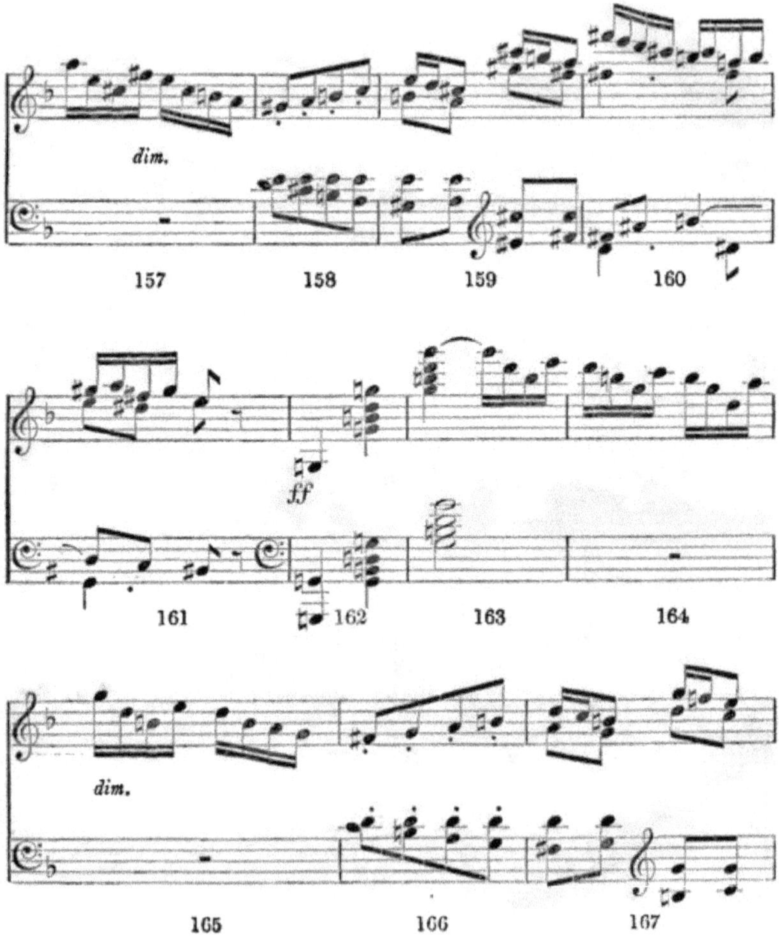
dim.
157
158
159
160
ff
161
162
163
164
dim.
165
166
167

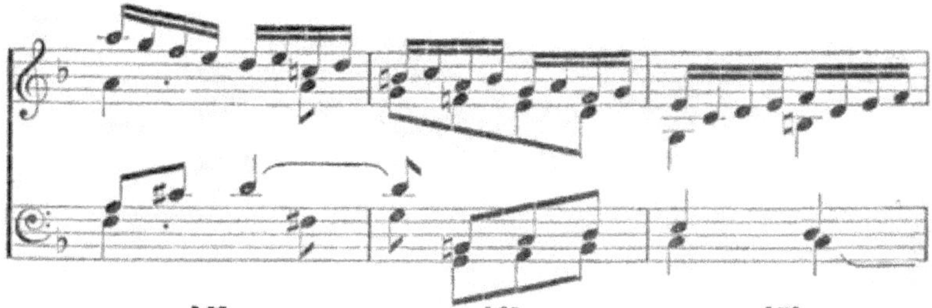
168
169
170

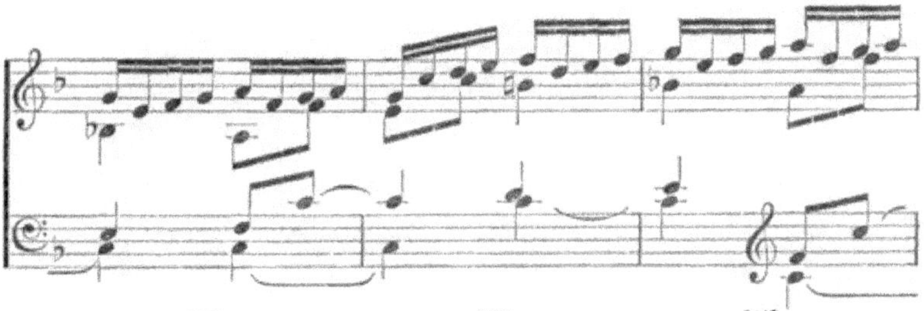
171
172
173

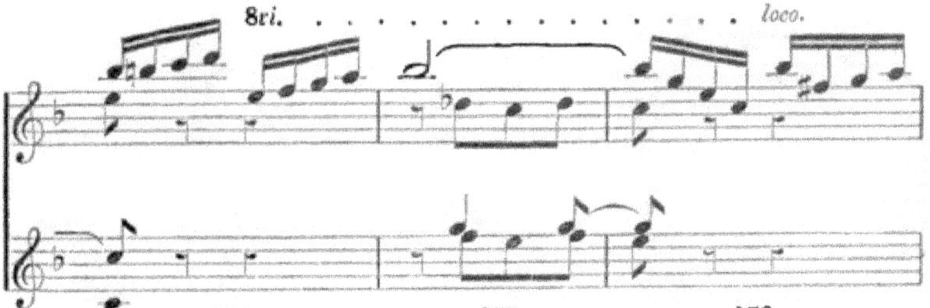
8vi.
loco.
174
175
176

riten.
177
178
179
180
a tempo.
mez.
181
182
183
184
8vi. . . . .
cres.
185
186
187

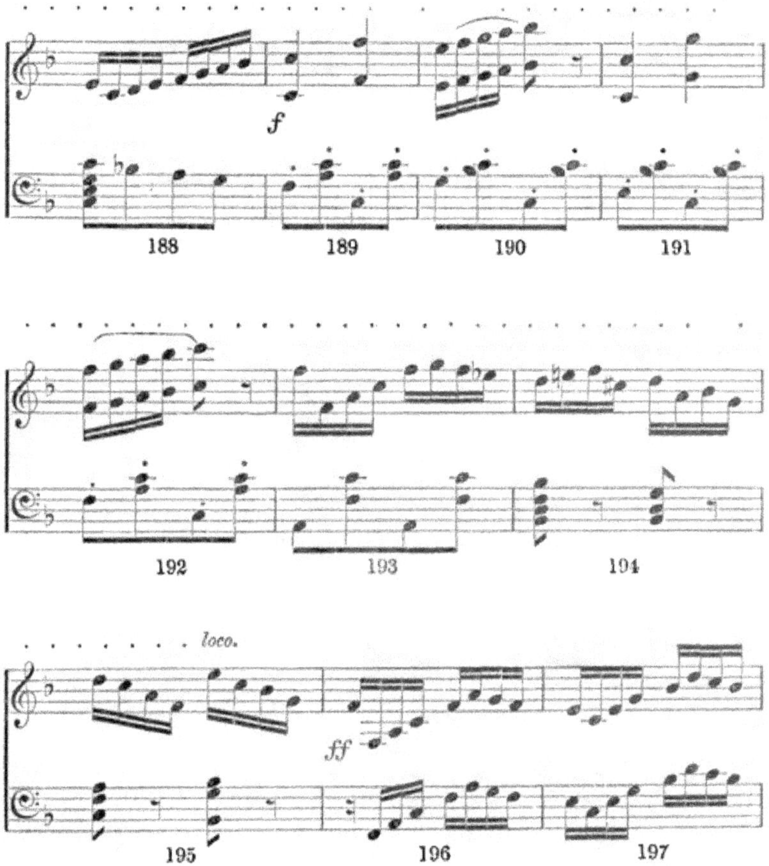
f
188
189
190
191
192
193
194
loco.
ff
195
196
197

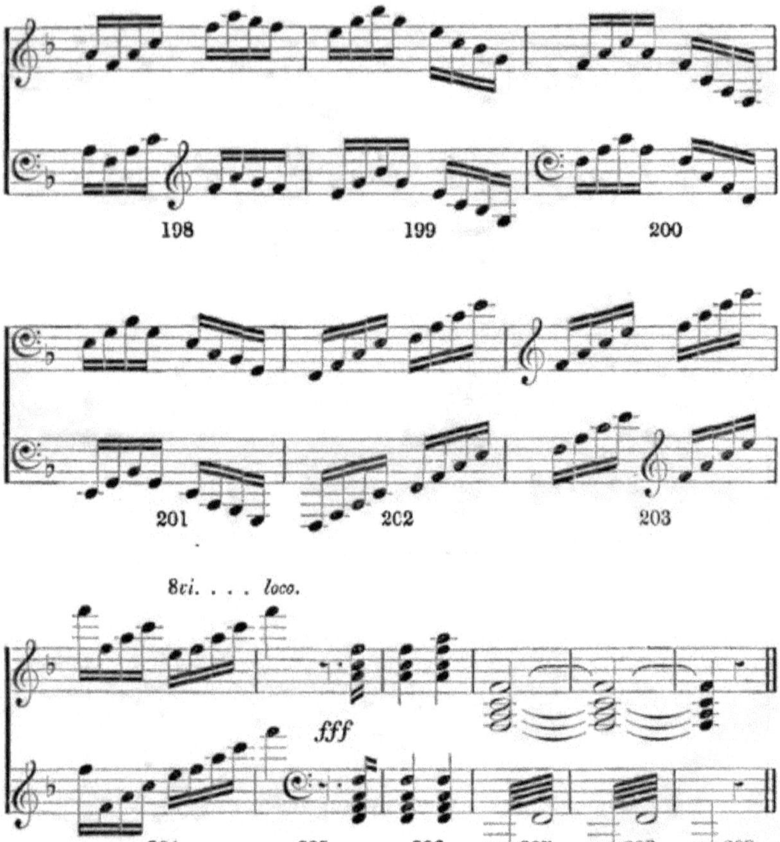
198
199
200
201
202
203
8vi. . . . loco.
fff
204
205
206
207
208
209

We would further recommend for study and analysis Beethoven's Septett, op. 20, which consists of the following movements, all very regular as to form, and beautiful as to melody, harmony, and instrumentation.

1. Introduction, in E flat major, 3-4.   Adagio.

2. Allegro con brio, in E flat major, **C**.   Modern binary form.

3. Adagio Cantabile, in A flat major, 9-8.   Modern binary form.

4. Minuet and Trio, in E flat major, 3-4.

5. Air with Variations, in B flat major, 2-4.   Andante.

6. Scherzo and Trio, in E flat major, 3-4.   Allegro Vivace.   Minuet form.

7. Introduction to Finale, in E flat minor, 2-4.   Andante con moto.

8. Finale, in E flat major, **¢**, Presto.   Modern Binary Form.

THE END.